TOKYO
A BIOGRAPHY

T0272881

The most effective way to destroy people is to deny and obliterate their own understanding of their history.
— George Orwell

…cities are not a collection of objects. Rather, they are a sequential continuum of sensory experiences.
— Edmund N. Bacon

STEPHEN MANSFIELD

TOKYO
A BIOGRAPHY

DISASTERS, DESTRUCTION AND RENEWAL:
THE STORY OF AN INDOMITABLE CITY

TUTTLE Publishing

Tokyo | Rutland, Vermont | Singapore

ABOUT TUTTLE
"Books to Span the East and West"

Our core mission at Tuttle Publishing is to create books which bring people together one page at a time. Tuttle was founded in 1832 in the small New England town of Rutland, Vermont (USA). Our fundamental values remain as strong today as they were then—to publish best-in-class books informing the English-speaking world about the countries and peoples of Asia. The world has become a smaller place today and Asia's economic, cultural and political influence has expanded, yet the need for meaningful dialogue and information about this diverse region has never been greater. Since 1948, Tuttle has been a leader in publishing books on the cultures, arts, cuisines, languages and literatures of Asia. Our authors and photographers have won numerous awards and Tuttle has published thousands of books on subjects ranging from martial arts to paper crafts. We welcome you to explore the wealth of information available on Asia at **www.tuttlepublishing.com**.

Published by Tuttle Publishing, an imprint of Periplus Editions (HK) Ltd.

www.tuttlepublishing.com

Copyright © 2016 by Stephen Mansfield

Library of Congress Cataloging-in-Publication Data is in progress

ISBN 978-4-8053-1329-9

First edition
19 18 17 16   5 4 3 2 1
1606CM

Printed in China

TUTTLE PUBLISHING® is a registered trademark of Tuttle Publishing, a division of Periplus Editions (HK) Ltd.

Distributed by

North America, Latin America & Europe
Tuttle Publishing
364 Innovation Drive
North Clarendon, VT 05759-9436 U.S.A.
Tel: 1 (802) 773-8930
Fax: 1 (802) 773-6993
info@tuttlepublishing.com
www.tuttlepublishing.com

Japan
Tuttle Publishing
Yaekari Building, 3rd Floor
5-4-12 Osaki, Shinagawa-ku
Tokyo 141 0032
Tel: (81) 3 5437-0171
Fax: (81) 3 5437-0755
sales@tuttle.co.jp
www.tuttle.co.jp

Asia Pacific
Berkeley Books Pte. Ltd.
61 Tai Seng Avenue, #02-12
Singapore 534167
Tel: (65) 6280-1330
Fax: (65) 6280-6290
inquiries@periplus.com.sg
www.periplus.com

Contents

This book is dedicated to
my son Rupert.

Preface

"It was in Rome, on the 15th of October, 1764," the great English historian Edward Gibbon wrote, "as I sat musing amidst the ruins of the Capitol, while the bare-footed friars were singing vespers in the Temple of Jupiter, that the idea of writing the decline and fall of the city first started in my mind." Few writers experience such timely or decisive moments. Cities creep up on us over time, insinuating themselves as an idea.

Gibbon's approach to history was to understand it in predominantly human terms. It was a view of the past that was free from the idea of any inherent purpose. History consisted of causes, effects, events; there were no determining laws, theorems, no divine purpose. It was the opposite of the view held by the classic Chinese historians, who saw history as preordained but manageable by decree—if the Mandate of Heaven was lost by a weak or corrupt ruler, he could be legitimately, justifiably usurped, and the whole process of history restarted. Gibbon, a man of the Enlightenment, demonstrated that there were other routes back into historical time. To retrace those routes was to reencounter the human footprint on time. It was in something akin to that spirit, and a desire to write a history that would include everything of significance and interesting insignificance, that this book was written.

Many accounts of Tokyo, even those created today, when we should know better, are surprisingly dated inversions of reality. These books all too often portray Tokyo as a city suffering from a multiple personality disorder, a city whose residents experience spasms rather than emotions. In foreign-made films with Tokyo settings, the actors wander the city like humans exploring the surface of Neptune. In one book, writer Paul Theroux dismisses Tokyo as "more like a machine than a city." This book was partly written as a riposte to the perception of Tokyoites as involuntary cells or charged particles streaming through the body of the city. Tokyo exists, like all great cities, because of the presence of a highly individual populace.

For any writer contemplating the past, the foremost question must be how to authentically render the historical experience, how to acquaint today's readers with yesterday's events. —How, in the case of Tokyo, to reconstruct time past in this least mnemonic of cities. When you start to think of the past as *happening*, as opposed to *having happened*, a new way of conceiving history becomes possible.

Despite its colossal building projects, Tokyo can still seem inchoate, even incorporeal, a massive jellyfish of cement and light. So great is the intensity of change that the city at times seems completely severed from its own history. There is no such thing, however, as an abiding city. The pattern, with rare exceptions, is invariably one of transformation, mutability. This is of course, a question of degree. Any talk of the past presupposes the persistence of history. Yet in Tokyo, we are presented with the very opposite: the *impersistence* of the past. Nothing is preordained. History is time travel.

Edward Seidensticker famously wrote that the argument between tradition and change—a characteristic of European cities—is less relevant in Tokyo, where change is a tradition. Considering all that has befallen the city, from natural disasters to the obliteration of Tokyo during World War II and the elimination of history in the postwar construction period, it is surprising that among the many sacred figures absorbed from India into the iconography of Japanese devotion Kali, the Hindu goddess of chaos and destruction, was not given a place among the city's pantheon of deities.

No doubt, some of the best city histories are impartial accountings, but if we make a cult out of impartiality, the result will be narrative leached of vitality. I've tried to strike a balance between objectivity for the sake of accuracy and, to borrow a term from Susan Sontag, the "passionate partiality" that comes from direct experience.

I can bear witness in small part to the city's recent history. I count myself lucky to have been on the platform at Kasumigaseki Station just hours before the sarin gas attack was carried out by a Japanese death cult. I was in the city when the earthquake and tsunami struck nearby Fukushima on March 3, 2011. I was fortunate to have gotten a sleeping unit on the upper floor of a twelve-story capsule hotel, the narrow building swaying drunkenly with the series of aftershocks. There was precious little sleep to be had that night. The capsule next to mine was occupied by a distressed insomniac babbling prophesies about a ruined city, like a biblical figure speaking in tongues.

The Asakusa Kannon temple, also called Senso-ji, may be the oldest religious site in the city, built to enshrine a gold statue of Kannon, Goddess of Mercy, that was "caught" by two fisherman on the Sumida River. Originally founded in 645, the temple was destroyed during the bombings of World War II. Once rebuilt it became, if possible, even more meaningful to the people of Tokyo as a symbol of compassion and peace. (Dreamstime © Zheng Dong)

Introduction

The flocks of *Grus japonensis*, the red-crowned crane, wading unmolested in the winter salt flats and tidal marshes, were not alone among avians nesting or sojourning along the swampy inlets of the bay. There were kestrels, egrets, Mongolian plovers, curlews, hawfinches, and the Japanese crested ibis, but it was the migratory crane—omnivorous consumer of crabs, snails, salamanders, and dragonflies—that would acquire special distinction as a Taoist symbol of immortality and fidelity, before it, too, like the city destined to rise here, would pass through cycles of growth, near-extinction, and transformation.

One thing that has not substantially changed is Tokyo's geology. The city sits on the Kanto Loam Stratum, a bed of hard red clay amassed in the aftermath of volcanic eruptions. Tokyo's topsoil of ash is roughly 20 meters deep. Abundant lashings of rain from the East Asian monsoons created sinkholes and depressions, forming sudden valleys in an otherwise flat terrain. The undulating unevenness—combined with the perforation caused by rivers and subterranean streams disgorging into pools, wetlands, and the bay—formed the crooked backstreets that follow the course of old, long-filled-in rivulets or subterranean streams faintly sensed in the low rumbling heard beneath storm drains and manholes, representing visible traces of a natural topography around which the city has evolved.

This much we can verify, yet the fog of time obscures history. Even the skeletons and fossils of prehistoric creatures, like the one of a Naumann elephant excavated from beneath the business center of Nihonbashi Hancho, represent a period of history as firmly interred in the past as these bone relics. With the development of implements like stone axes, knives, and hot pebbles used for cooking—which took place during the last glaciation some 20,000 to 30,000 years ago—large creatures like the elk and elephant became extinct. Colder gusts of air caused the earth to dry and then harden, then to experience tidal advances in the early Jomon period (8,000 BC–300 AD), when the climate once again grew warm, the shoreline reaching as far as the range of modest hills known today as the *yamanote*. The bluffs and ridges at the shore provided natural jetties for fishing and gathering shellfish. Shell mounds and the outlines of pit dwellings in present-day Itabashi and Kita wards, along with the discovery of stone tools along the upper banks of rivers and at the head of the bay, indicate the existence of primitive settlements, the home of Paleolithic hunter-gatherers.

A rich, inventive earthenware culture arose as the glacial epoch receded and a more temperate climate emerged. Earthen vessels from this period bear the impression of straw twines and cords pressed into the soft clay. These "cord-marked" pieces of pottery lent the age its name; the Jomon period. Tokyo is littered with mounds where these mollusk gatherers, a hunting, fishing, and gathering race, dumped their used shells. Bone tools and stone and ceramic ware have been found in middens.

As a study, archeology in Japan began, improbably, with the arrival of American zoologist Edward S. Morse, who visited to conduct advanced research on brachiopods, the Western Pacific shellfish. Traveling by train from Yokohama to Shimbashi on June 19, 1877, he chanced to glance out of the window as his carriage passed through the district of Omori. There he spotted a rise in the ground that he immediately identified as a shell mound. Further excavations revealed the site to be a 5,000-year-old Bronze Age cockleshell heap. Morse returned some days later with students from Tokyo Imperial University, and the group dug through the site with their bare hands, finding a "large collection of unique forms of pottery, three worked bones, and a curious baked-clay tablet." Similar kitchen heaps were found in Ochanomizu, on Ueno Hill, and even in the grounds of the present-day Imperial Palace. A thirst for knowledge led to more excavations and the unearthing, in 1884, of another stratum of Japanese history along a slope near present-day Nezu Station now known as Yayoi-zaka. Grains of charred rice and chaff were found in jars and pots by the student excavators, the discovery driving back the presumed date of the region's earliest agronomists.

The Yayoi period (300 BC–300 AD) was a time when rice cultivation and metalworking evolved in Japan. Advancements in better-managed communities during this period are visible in the everyday objects of the age. These include animal snares, fire pits, stronger earthen vessels fired at higher temperatures, clay figurines, lacquer ware, copper and iron tools, and burial urns—this latter an important and telling item. When people begin to honor their dead, they have made a significant leap in social development; the remembrance of ancestors is an important act in the establishing of historical time. The orange-brown-colored *haniwa* that were placed at the foot of ancient tumuli were also associated with remembrance of the dead. These unglazed clay figurines in cylindrical or configured forms represent people, animals, and familiar objects and shapes such as appliances and scale models of primitive residences.

In the western suburb of Todoroki, the scallop-shaped Noge Otsuka tomb has been preserved in remarkably fine condition. Dating from the fifth century, the mound is representative of the Middle Kofun culture that prevailed in the Kanto region. The hill is encircled with river stones and *haniwa*. Excavations of its one stone and two wooden coffins revealed a trove of relics, including swords, iron arrowheads, armor, armlets, iron sickles, bronze mirrors, and combs. The quality of the relics and the scale of the tomb indicate that this was the resting place of a powerful chieftain based in the southern Musashino area. The keyhole-shaped Horaisan Kofun, in nearby Tamagawa, is Tokyo's oldest tomb, dating from the fourth century. Its burial relics attest to the existence of a ruler who controlled much of the Tama River region.

If geography and climate define habitat, it was inevitable that people would settle within the eight provinces that made up the Kanto plain. The largest region of flatland in Japan, its location on the eastern seaboard placed it at the furthest distance from potential enemies invading from continental Asia. As it was well-irrigated, it was ideal for the cultivation of rice and for the training of horses in the employ of warriors.

The site of the villages from which Tokyo would emerge straddles three rivers—the Sumida, the Arakawa, and the Edogawa—as they flow over the flat alluvial lowland before discharging into Tokyo Bay. This broad swath of land, barely above sea level, is highly prone to flooding and other disasters; it has been the subject of countless calamities and will likely be so again. Much of the shore was marshy, but when the area was developed in the late sixteenth century, land reclamation projects solidified the shoreline, adding space to the future city.

As river courses altered and geological shifts and changes in sea levels occurred, upland plains formed. The biggest landmass of this sort is the Musashino plateau, a diluvial plain running 60 kilometers west of the city center to the mountainous edges of the Kanto plain. Its escarpments penetrate into the city, creating a clearly defined geography separating the flat, low-lying sections of the city close to the bay and river estuaries called the *shitamachi* (low city) from the rising inland zones called the *yamanote* (high city). The zonal distinction extends far beyond geography.

The areas comprising present-day Tokyo were not entirely uninhabited; early Korean communities were said to have settled along the Sumida River. On March 18 in the year 628—a surprisingly concise date—an event took place that would presage the rise of a city that was not just martial, but also devotional. Hinokuma Takenari and his brother Hamanari, both fishermen, found a small gold statue of Kannon, the Goddess of Mercy, tangled in their nets. According to the story, they threw the image back into the river, only to witness it reappear. When the image was taken to their liege, Haji-no-Nakatomo, he interpreted the incident as auspicious, and built a hall in his home to enshrine the deity. Completed in 645, the Asakusa Kannon temple may be the oldest religious site in the city. The diminutive statue became a *hibutsu*, a hidden image—one too sacred to set eyes on. The origin of the icon remains a mystery, but a possible explanation surfaced in 1945, just after the firebombing of the temple, when the remains of the main hall were being excavated. Religious implements and tiles of continental Asian origin dating from the seventh and eighth century were found, hinting at the possibility that the statue is of Korean provenance.

The flatness of the Musashino plateau, in a country where mountains are revered, seems to have inspired despondent thoughts, its very vastness a limitation, as this ancient poem implies:

> The Musashino plain,
> Where there are few mountains
> For the moon to approach.
> Rising gibbous from the loam,
> It sinks back into the grass.

The twelve-year-old Lady Sarashino crossed the Sumida River one gusty autumn day in 1020, noting, as her entourage was swallowed up by the expanse of grasses, that the reeds were so tall that the "very tips of the horsemen's bows were invisible." The principal characteristic of the plain—its dense overgrowth of grasses, pampas, wild bush clover, and reeds—was documented over the centuries in poetry. Clear skies, the moon, and Mount Fuji—easily visible from the plain—were subjects of a number of later paintings. In one pair of six-fold screens created by an unknown artist in the seventeenth century, a tangle of wild carnations, wild grasses, and Chinese bellflowers occupies the foreground.

By the twelfth century, a medieval society was beginning to emerge, with the samurai military class taking the reins of power from an incompetent, inward-looking bureaucratic aristocracy in Kyoto. The name "Edo" seems to have first been used around this time, when Chichibu Shigetsugu built a home on a section of tableland at Kojimachi, naming himself after the location. His name change—he was thenceforth called Edo Shigetsugu—marks the first historical reference to the place-name Edo. (Edo meant "door to the cove," an indicator of how far Tokyo Bay penetrated into the center of the city, its waters lapping up against the shore of the Kojimachi tableland.)

Present-day Tokyo, then part of the eastern provinces, belonged to the Koku domain of Musashino, the *koku-fu* (provincial capital) based in the present-day city of Fuchu. Stretches of the wild, lonely plain were not always safe for travelers or pilgrims. The thirteenth-century bandit Owada Dogen earned a reputation for waylaying travelers passing through an overgrown valley as they progressed westward toward the mountains. His name has survived in a road in the Shibuya district called Dogen-zaka, a slope that now bears little resemblance to the one haunted by the city's most notorious highwayman.

As these accounts demonstrate, history preserved in names, sufficing for the absence of any material evidence of the past, was to become a characteristic of a city thoroughly fixated on the present.

Hagoita—small wooden paddles used in a New Year's game called *hanetsuki*—are usually decorated with the faces of *kabuki* characters. The game, which is something like badminton, is hardly played any more, but the Hagoita Market continues to be a New Year tradition at the Senso-ji temple—one that dates back about 350 years. The faces of *kabuki* characters can still be seen in theatrical performances; the art form endures to this day. (Dreamstime © Meaothai)

CHAPTER 1

The Master Plan

Fishing village to citadel – Social structure – First
foreign visitors – Pleasure quarters – Flowers of Edo

The origins of entire dynasties have been predicated on founda-
tion myths, cities on oracular prophesies, the divinations of occult
figures, the occurrence and mediation of supra-human incidents.
Accordingly, legend claims that the goddess Benten, through the
medium of a fish that leapt out of the river, led the feudal lord
Ota Dokan to a low hill where he was commanded to erect a fortress in the vicinity of a nondescript fishing village named Edo.

The mound, standing above the outer gardens of today's Imperial Palace, was easily defensible, commanding the estuaries of
a number of local rivers. One of those waterways was the Hibiya
inlet, connected to Edo Bay. Boats could anchor at a quay near
the foot of the settlement. Under Ota's supervision, beginning
in 1457, the quay was turned into a thriving center for shipping
and trade. Fish, rice, tea, copper, iron, and much-coveted herbal
medicines from China were offloaded here.

Visiting poets, scribes and members of the literary nobility
left short accounts of this first incarnation of the city, but no
trace remains of its earth fortifications or structures. Its thatched
buildings, compacted earthen embankments, bamboo palisades,

ditches, and wells were likely more akin to a rural stockade than a castle. The site reverted to nature and the original fishing families who predated the settlement after Ota Dokan's murder in 1486 at the command of his own lord, Uesugi Sadamasa, who was jealous of Ota's success as a military strategist and gifted administrator.

The plot of land rose to unexpected prominence a hundred years later. Its elevation from a dismal fishing village huddled within marshland to the world's largest city begins with the arrival of the warrior-clan head Tokugawa Ieyasu in 1590. The site of Edo and its eight surrounding provinces were Ieyasu's reward for masterminding a successful military campaign against the Hojo clan, the principal rivals of the supreme hegemon Toyotomi Hideyoshi, who had occupied the fiefdom and overseen it from his stronghold at Odawara. Hideyoshi's largesse concealed a desire to distance Ieyasu from Kyoto and the centers of power. The offer, a disguised banishment, was finalized during the fall of Hojo castle. At the suggestion of Ieyasu, the promise was sealed by the two of them urinating in unison in the direction of Odawara—perhaps the only example in history of the fate of a location destined to become a world-class city being sealed with the simultaneous relieving of bladders.

It took a visionary to see abundant promise in the mosquito-infested salt inlets and reedy swamps at the head of the long bay where Ieyasu would build his bastion. Geography may be destiny, but shared perceptions cannot be assumed. The two men's visions of Edo could not have been more different: Hideyoshi judged the under populated wetlands to be a godforsaken place with a deficit of natural spring water; Ieyasu envisaged a dazzling new city, a civil and military citadel encircled by a great bay fed by a system of navigable rivers.

Ieyasu, in common with other authoritarian city-builders the world over, possessed the mind of an engineer. Casting an eye over the worm-eaten fishing huts, salt-eroded port structures, termite-infested storehouses, and decaying steps to the main gate of Ota's soot-blackened fortress, Ieyasu saw immense promise, visualizing the infrastructure of a great city where others saw only a morass. Even the moderately astute could see some advantages to a site at the entrance to the Kanto plain that had sea access and was near the estuaries of Japan's greatest waterway in the east, the Tone River. Located at the top of the bay, the site would be easy to defend, and was less vulnerable to storms than other sea-facing settlements like nearby Kamakura.

After winning the Battle of Sekigahara in 1600, Ieyasu emerged as shogun from the power struggle that had ensued after Hideyoshi's death in 1598. Ieyasu was unchallenged in his control of the entire country, leaving a powerless emperor and effete court to their own distractions in Kyoto. His first official entry into the city may have occurred as early as the summer of 1590; he would have passed his first night in a Buddhist temple, at that time a common form of lodging for high-ranking visitors. The endorsement of the new city and its military regime by Shinto and Buddhist priests was considered crucial to the legitimacy of the city. Like those of the pagan priests of Rome, their services—which included dedicatory rites, funereal proceedings, and important consecrations—accorded the priests a status only a little below that of the warrior class.

It was important for Ieyasu that the physical structure of Edo replicate the hierarchical social order of what would arguably become the most well-managed feudal society the world has ever known. The master plan required strict social and occupational classes: peasants, artisans, and merchants. The members of one class could not legally intermarry with members of another class; nor, at least in theory, could they change their occupations.

Below the house-owning merchant families and the service class who rented property were outcast groups known as *eta* and *hinin*. Discrimination extended to the districts in which they were permitted to live; these were well removed from the daimyo and samurai. Clothing and hairstyles were required to be functional, understated. Outcasts lived in hamlets on the periphery of the city, engaging in the most onerous tasks: working in slaughter houses, curing animal hides, digging ditches, disposing of the dead, assisting in torture chambers and at the execution grounds. Others eked out a living as street performers, fortunetellers, blind musicians, and wandering mendicants.

The 176 *fudai daimyo* (inside lords) who had risked their estates and livelihoods by supporting Ieyasu even in the days before his victory at Sekigahara were allocated choice parcels of land to build estates on within the shadow of Edo Castle; the *tozama daimyo* (outer lords), the eighty-six noblemen not prescient enough to ally themselves with Ieyasu, were to reside in more peripheral zones, where allegiance and its concomitant compliance became a form of survival. An inability to trust one's own subjects—a characteristic of all dictatorships—was reflected in a complicated system called *sankin kotai* (alternative residence). This required all daimyo to maintain two residencies: one in Edo, the other in their home province. One year was to be spent at the Edo residence, the next at their domain. The divide-and-rule approach was reinforced by the stipulation that half of the outer lords had to make their return to Edo in March every year, while the other half returned to their ancestral homes at the same time. The inside lords did the same in August. The processions marking their departure and return required costly displays of pomp and ostentation. A further proviso required daimyo to leave their consorts, children and heirs apparent permanently in their Edo residencies as a warranty against insurrection. For good measure, the shogunate erected barriers along the main routes into Edo, enforcing a "no women out, no weapons in" rule.

Obliging the daimyo to live in grand style while in Edo, to build residences in a style reflecting the more sumptuous tastes of the earlier Momoyama era, and to maintain large retinues and staff ensured they did not have sufficient funds to purchase arms and mount an insurgency. In the most effective tradition of menace, the real purpose of alternative residence was never spelled out, but implicitly understood. The system firmly established Edo—as opposed to the imperial capital of Kyoto—as the country's de facto seat of governance, and therefore an unassailable military citadel.

The obsession with security and the determination to build a fortress impregnable to any potential assailant dictated that steep walls be used to face the raised ground above the moats surrounding the citadel. The granite and volcanic rock used in the construction of the elevated embankments came from the Izu peninsula, some 85 kilometers south of Edo. Carried by ships, some three thousand all told, the rocks were offloaded at the dock and then dragged by rotating teams of laborers and ox carts. Seaweed was placed under the larger stones to facilitate their movement, and itinerant musicians blowing conches, banging drums, and dancing in a comedic parody of "southern barbarians" (as Europeans were called) were employed to spur on the work.

The castle's inner ramparts consisted of massive walls of stone curving outward in graceful convex lines from moats. Pine trees, planted at the top of the fortifications, were carefully trained to lean downward over the curving masonry and the water's surface. The medina of water channels, tidewater moats, estates, and alleys formed both an auspicious and physically protective cosmos with the castle at the gravitational center. The impregnability of the castle was never tested, but the plans show a structure that was as impervious as any Saracen fortress or Cathar stronghold.

Being the central topographical feature of the early city, the castle was also its nerve center, a structure whose centrality to the life of the city was highlighted by its strategic positioning. The primacy of Edo Castle—which was finally completed in 1640— was emphasized in maps of the city: it was always shown at the center, occupying Edo's most elevated ground. The prestige of place and site names, usually written vertically, were reflected in the location and direction of the ideograms used on the maps to represent them. Thus the higher status of Buddhist temples and shrines means that, cartographically speaking, they were shown facing toward the castle. Likewise, private residences and shops were depicted facing away from the castle in accordance with their status.

The form of the castle and its protective moats resembled a logarithmic spiral. This shape is associated with a mystical form in Shinto originating from the Taoist yin-yang, the harmony of opposites that underpins the functioning of the universe. The design of Edo Castle and its environs may have favored the circular to fortify an unassailable political system, but the directions—the energy flows of the city—were far from centrifugal. Chinese geomancy dictated how principles, symbols, and directions should influence the auspicious placement of buildings. The troublesome east, direction of the Cyan Dragon, required a waterway; this was provided by the Sumida River. The west, domain of the White Tiger, demanded a major highway—one already in place in the form of the Tokaido trunk road. The south, provenance of the Vermillion Bird, required a pond. This called for a little more creative thinking, but a surrogate was found in the waters of Edo Bay. A mountain was mandatory for the northerly direction, habitat of the Dark Warrior, but the only option was Mount Fuji in the west. This problem was solved by reorienting the castle's main gate, the Ote-mon, from the south to the east. If the fortress were read as a compass, the sacred peak could be understood to occupy the northern coordinate. Geomancy dictated that on maps, Edo had to be oriented (rotated more than 90 degrees counter-clockwise) so that Mount Fuji's actual west-southwest orientation would correspond with Gembu, the god of the north.

Geomantic concerns continued to occupy the thoughts of subsequent shoguns in their desire to reinforce the city against malevolent forces. In 1624, the second shogun, Hidetaka, asked the influential priest Tenkai to construct a temple in the northeast quarter of Ueno. Both the quarter and the cardinal point were believed to be the source from which evil flowed. To block this portal, known as the Kimon (Devil's Gate), Tenkai constructed Kan'ei-ji temple. Successive shoguns continued developing the barrier; by 1700, there were no fewer than thirty-six sub-temples in the area.

The diagonal flow of malign forces required a temple counterpart to Kan'ei-ji in the southeast. In accordance with these beliefs, the great Zojo-ji, a temple of the Jodo sect, was established in Shiba in 1598. At its height it must have been a magnificent complex, with forty-eight sub-temples and over a hundred structures in all. On completion, the mausoleums of the Tokugawa shoguns lined each side of the temple. Their compounds were replete with the lacquered gates and carved and painted transoms, eaves, and beams attesting to the Tokugawa love of elaboration. These features are evident not only in their private residences and art collections, but also in the great shrine and mausoleum that would be built for the shogun Ieyasu at Nikko in Tochigi Prefecture.

Both sets of daimyo—the favored and the disgraced—were expected to supply labor, funds, and materials for the construction of ambitious projects, particularly the building of Edo Castle, a project that would take several more decades to complete. Compliance was considered a test of allegiance. In a city built by fiat, policy was made by diktat; advice, when it was solicited, was taken exclusively from the inside lords and those close to them, deemed infallible loyalists. The Hibiya inlet, at the eastern edge of the castle site, was filled in with earth taken from the Surugadai hill in Kanda to the north. Impressive feats of engineering, which involved diverting water channels and rivers to form a spiderweb of canals and an inner and outer moat, were required to complete the system. The Kanda River was co-opted as a source of water for the moats surrounding the castle, a function it still serves today. Landfills were created by removing earth from the high terrain of the Yamanote hills to the north and west. A waterway known as the Dosanbori Canal was dug to enable the transportation of construction materials. Ieyasu used the construction as a way to test the loyalty of his supporters and as a further attempt to deplete the coffers of suspected rivals by demanding massive outlays from them in material resources as well as assignments of corvée labor. This was all part of a colossal civil engineering project called *tenka-fushin* (construction of the realm).

With the circulation of waterways for transport and security determined, the practical business of providing a flow of potable water for Edo became an immediate priority. Early attempts to bore wells in the coastal city had only succeeded in drawing up salt water. The Kanda Josui, a 17-kilometer water system, consisted of more than 3,600 sub-aqueducts. The subterranean sections used pipes made from hollowed-out timber to transport water to communal wells. The system was operational by the Kan'ei era (1624–44). It was an admirable system, far superior to many of the appalling water management arrangements in contemporaneous European cities, but with the rapid expansion of Edo the Kanda Josui soon reached capacity.

In 1652 in the western district of Tama, where villagers were already engaged in manufacturing lime for construction projects, work began on a second water system, the Tamagawa Josui. On its completion two years later, the 80-kilometer-long system was able to carry fresh water to every part of the city. Further measures were taken to improve the quality of water supplied to Edo, including the removal of crudely made latrines and huts along riverbanks and prohibitions against the disposal of waste in rivers.

Once matters like the benign flow of spiritual forces and the redirection of water had been settled, city planners turned their attention to the flow of human traffic. The *sankin kotai* system of alternative residence meant that the approach roads to Edo were always busy, requiring greater numbers of post-stations near the city. Shinjuku had its Koshu-kaido trunk road to the west, Senju the Nikko-kaido running north. Some of the country's major highways spread out radially from within the moat: the Tokaido in the south, the Daisendo to the southwest, the Koshu-kaido to the west, and the Nakasendo to the northeast. The superimposition of moats and highways at the center was one of the most distinct features of the city. The improved transportation systems not only freed up space for daimyo entourages, but also facilitated the movement of officials, merchants, goods, and the increasing volume of people making pilgrimages to holy sites.

The residences of daimyo and samurai families took up a disproportionate 70 percent of Edo's land disposition. Land occupied by temples and shrines accounted for roughly 14 percent of the city, leaving only a 16 percent residential allocation for commoners, a demographically far larger group, to build their homes and shops. Many increasingly prosperous merchant families were able to do this, but the fate of Edo's service class was to rent row houses in the back streets and alleys of the city.

Typically, these *ura nagaya*, or "rear long-houses," were partitioned into units with living areas seldom larger than 3 meters square. A narrow cooking space and entrance added an extra strip of flooring at a slightly lower elevation than the main floor. An entire family might live in this single room. A large number of single men, supporting families in the countryside, occupied these homes. Most of these bachelor tenants were of the lower orders, scraping out a living as mendicant entertainers, laborers, and tinkers—though there were among them *ronin* (masterless samurai) fallen on hard times. Communal facilities included garbage dumps, the toilet, and the well where the washing and laundry were done. Rats were drawn to the garbage piles and the runnels that served as open sewers running along the middle of the alleys, where in some cases the width between the clapboard residences was less than a meter. Sleeping conditions inside the row houses must have been suffocating. Within the confined space, the superheated air—particularly in the humid summer evenings, when lamps powered by rapeseed oil and vegetable wax were used—would have been stifling. There was no special night-wear; people slept in their daytime clothes.

An abundance of water, an asset in normal times, could exacerbate sanitation problems. In a normal year the Sumida River could be expected to flood twice, its inundations turning districts along its banks into quagmires of foul-smelling mud. Canals, pools, and puddles were the perfect breeding ground for the swarms of mosquitoes that infested the city in the summer months. Insects and rodents swarmed at the unwholesome fish markets. In such conditions, it is little wonder that epidemics of diseases like measles, smallpox, and beriberi were so common. The latter, caused largely by the nutritional deficiencies inherent to an unvaried diet of polished white rice, was so persistent it was dubbed the "Edo disease."

The two-story homes of the wealthy merchants, shopkeepers, and occasional winners of temple lotteries, whose frontages onto wider streets provided better access and light, were far superior. Their tiled roofs were somewhat fire-resistant; their earthen surfaces were covered in a burnt ash from crushed oyster shells, India ink, and lime. With time and wear, the dark stucco and plaster walls became so lustrous that the sight of women stopping to adjust their hair in front of the semi-reflective surfaces was not uncommon. Though they were despised as money-grubbers by the aristocracy and warrior class, merchants were a vital element, as they provisioned the city.

In 1606, one of Ieyasu's first acts as shogun had been to order the creation of a camellia garden within the castle grounds (site of the current Ninomaru Garden). The moist air, plentiful rainfall, and generous parcels of land allotted to daimyo were perfect for the creation of aristocratic "stroll gardens." Ponds were excavated for these artificial landscapes. At high tide they would fill with salt water; at low tide their levels were controlled by sluice gates. Some of these—like the Hama-Rikyu and Kyu Shiba-Rikyu Onshi gardens—remain, though in diminished scale.

Less pleasing to the eye were Edo's execution grounds. Executions were generally conducted at the city prison in Kodenmacho, while burning at the stake and crucifixions were confined to the Suzugamori execution ground near Shinagawa, where some 150,000 criminals were dispatched. Criminals were placed backward on a horse, paraded around the city, then tied to a wooden cross, a practice that continued into the mid-nineteenth century. They would then be speared through the side in crucifixion scenes not unlike the one on the hill at Golgotha in the Christian bible. A pyre where bodies were burnt alive and a stone platform for impalings remain as testament to the public staging of punishments. The execution grounds were located beside the Tokaido trunk road to remind travelers of the fate of those whose criminal acts made them outcasts unworthy of a decent interment in the family grave at a temple.

Another execution ground existed at Kotsukappara, an area in the northeast of the city near Minami Senju and the day-labor district of Sanya. More than 200,000 severed heads were reportedly displayed on stakes here. Shortly after the establishment of Kotsukappara in 1651, a statue of Jizo—patron of stillborn children, travelers, and souls suffering in hell—was erected to stand guard over the grounds; the figure is known as the "Chopped-neck Jizo." Kotsukappara was a benighted place, characterized by a bleakness and dereliction that still clings, like the reek of a tomb, to some of the back streets and alleys of the district. Disposing of dead bodies—whether of criminals or ordinary citizens—fell to the outcast *hinin* and *eta*. Their descendants, now referred to in hushed undertones as *burakumin* (hamlet people), continue to inhabit present-day districts to the east of the city such as Taito, Arakawa, and Sumida wards, where there are concentrations of the small factories, crematoriums, and leather-working shops in which work traditionally assigned to untouchable groups is carried out.

An antidote to such grim sights, Mount Fuji stands a hundred kilometers southeast of Nihonbashi. In the perspective-compressing prints of the day it appears as a looming presence, the principal feature in the Edo landscape. The city's close links to the mountain were partly due to its powerful symbolism: the mountain was the locus of a complex mix of beliefs and doctrines practiced by religious cults dedicated to its worship. Dominant among these quasi-religious sects during the early Edo period was Shugendo, or mountain asceticism. Reflecting Fuji's transcendent quality, the unquestioned notion that it was the most proximate peak to heaven, an inordinate number of shrines in Edo were dedicated to the deities that resided on the mountain. Each of these places of worship contained a miniature Mount Fuji within their grounds, where devotees, unable to make the pilgrimage to the real mountain, would climb and offer prayers. On "mountain-opening day" supplicants would offer prayers to the rising sun from these diminutive, easily scaled peaks.

Tokugawa Ieyasu died in 1616—the same year as William Shakespeare—having, like the bard, accomplished a great deal in his lifetime. By the 1650s Edo's population had reached almost half a million, making it the largest city in Japan. Among the immigrants from other cities and the countryside were a small number of foreigners, the first overseas visitors to Japan since the arrival of early Chinese Buddhists. Dutch traders, restricted to a tiny artificial island known as Dejima in Nagasaki, were subjected to every possible humiliation in order to maintain their trade. Annual delegations to Edo were required between 1660 and 1790; thereafter, tributary visits were made every four years. Having visited Edo in the 1690s, Engelbert Kaempfer, a German naturalist and physician in the employ of the Dutch East India Company, gave a detailed account of the strange obeisance required of foreign visitors when they made their mandatory annual visit to Edo Castle in his *History of Japan*, posthumously published in 1727:

> The moment the captain appeared, an affectedly loud
> voice called out, *"Oranda kapitan"* (Holland captain),
> a signal for him to step forward and pay his respects.

He was then expected to crawl forward on hands and knees to the spot where the presents brought by the Dutch were displayed, and to the high seat of the shogun. Crouching on his knees, he bent his head to the floor and then, like a lobster, crawled back, all this without one word being exchanged.

It was a tiresome business, but the Dutch, eager to stay in the good graces of the shogun and maintain their preeminence in trade, were grudgingly prepared to oblige.

On a less pantomimic note, the shogunate required the Dutch mission to submit an annual report on world events and developments beyond the confines of Japan. The Dutch duly obliged—an arrangement that continued until the end of the policy of national seclusion in the mid-nineteenth century.

In a set of four linked gold-leaf screens known as *Edo Meisho-zu Byobu* (Screens of Famous Places in Edo), now in the collection of the Idemitsu Museum of Art, we can gain some idea of how Edo looked at the time of the early Dutch tributary visits to the city. Besides Edo Castle, the screens depict a Noh performance, a ballad drama performed by *joruri* puppets used in epic narrative dramas, acrobats at a tent in the Shinbashi district, and scenes at an annual festival at the Senso-ji temple. It is a hyper-compression of reality that nevertheless reflects an already energetic, culturally virile city.

As the areas surrounding the citadel evolved into an urban center, two distinct communities of townspeople sprang up. The first of these was the *shiro-shitamachi*, an area of soon-to-be-affluent merchant stores and businesses centering on Nihonbashi and Kyobashi. Shirokiya, a large commodities store, opened in Nihonbashi in 1662, developing into a successful merchandizing chain that became today's Tokyu department store. Maps of the district from the mid-seventeenth century show a rectilinear grid system that would soon be overwhelmed by a far more organic and random urban evolution. The second area, which sprang up along the banks of the Sumida River, consisted in the main of small businesses and *shokunin* (craftsman) residences. The center of this area of intense activity was Asakusa, to the north of the original *shiro-shitamachi*.

Nihonbashi Bridge was the starting point for the Tokaido, the "Eastern Road" that ran to the imperial capital of Kyoto. Four major trunk roads originated at the bridge. Its zero marker remains even today the point from which all distances are measured. Bulletin boards were placed at the approaches to the bridge, making the spot an information outlet. Sexual offenders and adulterers, among whom an inordinate number appear to have been priests, were placed in fetters at the south end of the bridge. The public exposure and resulting humiliation effectively combined punishment and penitence. Murderers were buried alive with their heads protruding from the earth. A saw was conveniently placed nearby. Passersby, if so inclined, could pick up the tool and sever the head, which would then be placed on a pike at the end of the bridge. This terrifying apparition of death—rapidly decaying heads with their eyes gouged out by ravens—served as a powerful deterrent to potential felons.

The dry winter winds that the Kanto region is prone to, combined with all its wooden structures, made Edo especially fire-prone. The Meireki Fire, which broke out on the morning of January 18, 1657, was one of the era's most notable conflagrations, destroying almost two-thirds of the buildings in Edo. Better known as the Long Sleeves Fire, the conflagration started at an exorcism ceremony at Honmyo-ji temple in Hongo for a kimono that had been used by three young women who subsequently died prematurely. When a gale blew up during the ritual, embers from the costume settled on the roof of a nearby temple, setting off a sequence of fires that, fanned by powerful westerly winds, spread across the contiguous quarters of Yushima and Surugadai before moving on to ravage the districts of Nihonbashi, Tsukudajima, Kobikicho, and the important rice granaries in Asakusa. That fire burned out, but a second rose up in the samurai district of Koishikawa, going on to destroy Edo Castle and countless warrior residences. More fires flared up that evening in the Kojimachi quarter.

The fire penetrated the spacious grounds of Edo Castle, burning down the main keep and melting all the gold stock that was stored in its cellar. The interior walls of the castle, decorated with priceless paintings by the great court artist Kano Tanyu, were destroyed. Among the human casualties of the Long Sleeves Fire were the inmates of the city's main prison at Kodenmacho. Somehow, the understanding between the prisoners and the authorities that they would be released from the jail and meet up at an agreed temple location was muddled as the fires approached. The authorities, believing that prisoners were trying to escape and loot the city, had the gates firmly closed, resulting in the death of more than twenty thousand people.

In the two days of raging fires, 930 daimyo residences were razed and 350 temples and shrines were destroyed, along with 1,200 merchants' homes and 61 bridges. The estimated number of victims was 108,000 out of a population of 300,000. The timing was pitiless; the following day it snowed. Despite the prompt distribution of relief rice from the shogun's granaries, many people died from starvation and hypothermia.

If two detailed paintings on folded screens (the *Screen of Edo* and the *Screen of Famous Places in Edo*) and an early extant Kan'ei-era (1624–43) map of Edo are accurate, the city built after the fire was not as splendid as the castle town that preceded it. The ensuing reconstruction—based more on pragmatic concerns than aesthetics—required wider streets, firebreaks, and a program to get merchants to fireproof their homes and storehouses with plaster, which radically altered the appearance of the city. Carpenters, sawyers, and plasterers did well in this still largely flammable city. Burnt earth from the fire was collected and used to reclaim a number of marshes. Ryogoku-bashi, Edo's "Interstate Bridge," was built over the Sumida River, effectively annexing the east side of the city for further development. Lumberyards were moved from Hatchobori to Fukagawa, a supposedly less incendiary area east of the river. The transfer to Fukagawa, which at that point was little more than a marsh, added to the eastward movement and expansion of the *shitamachi*, more land reclamation, and the building of docks and storage yards. Preeminent lumber tycoons like Bunzaemon Kinokuniya made fortunes from the almost constant necessity to rebuild. The lumber king's own mansion was located a sensible distance from the river, so that fresh water could be channeled into the garden.

Rather than being cowed by the fire, the city took on a fresh life, actually expanding in size so that formerly rural areas now became part of the urban mass of Edo. Fires were the price you paid for living in the most culturally dynamic city in Japan. The ever-positive townspeople even chose to see poetic merit in the fires, calling the periodic conflagrations *Edo no hana*, the "flowers of Edo." Vigor flowed back into the veins of Edo citizens, their irrepressible energy at times usurping the best-laid plans of the authorities. No sooner had a large area of merchant houses between the bridges at Nihonbashi and at Edobashi been cleared to create a firebreak, for example, than food stalls, storytelling booths, makeshift tea houses, and tents putatively known as "archery ranges," which actually functioned as brothels, began to line the newly broadened Edobashi Road, nullifying the self-evident benefits of the project.

In a city so vulnerable to fire, it is not surprising to learn that arson was punishable by death. When a fire broke out in the winter of 1682 near the home of a greengrocer's daughter named Oshiichi, the family was forced to seek shelter in Enjo-ji, a nearby temple, where she fell secretly, fatally, in love with one of its young acolytes. Her family's shop was rebuilt and she reluctantly returned home, but impulsively set fire to her own house in the hopes of being sent back to the temple again. Instead, she was caught in the act and thrown into jail. Being just short of sixteen, she could have had the death penalty reduced to a life sentence. Unable to contemplate separation from the object of her love, however, she altered her age by one year and duly received the death sentence. Her comportment as she was led through the streets, unapologetic and seemingly unfazed by any concerns for the ghastly fate awaiting her at the execution ground at Suzugamori, won over the hearts of bystanders. Like those of many popular folk heroines, her story acquired extra details and embellishment with the passage of time.

To some degree, fires were also tied to the Buddhist concept of *ukiyo*, the "sorrowful world," referring to the grief-laden plane of existence defined by transience and impermanence. Reinterpreting the word homophonically, the Genroku-era (1688–1704) merchants and tradesmen who lived in this period of heightened affectation and dilettantism, which was contemporaneous with the Restoration in England, altered the meaning of *ukiyo* from "sorrowful world" to "floating world," suggesting a realm of sensual, hedonistic pleasures.

After the Meireki Fire, the authorities, who regarded the pleasure districts and the theatres as *akusho* (venues of moral degeneration), had the city's preeminent pleasure quarter, the Yoshiwara, removed from east of the castle to Asakusa in the northeast, where they hoped it would languish. To their chagrin, Asakusa's location on the banks of the Sumida River meant that an easy boat trip could be made up the river into the Sanya Canal and thence to the pleasure quarter. At Yanagibashi, the "Willow-Tree Bridge" located at the mouth of the Kanda River, boats known as *chokibune* could be boarded for that purpose; however, enterprising locals soon turned the water district into an unlicensed quarter, obviating the need for those with less refined tastes or funds to travel upriver to the Yoshiwara. For their part, brothel owners in the Yoshiwara were delighted that they were now allowed to stay open all night. This led to the quarter being dubbed the *fuyajo*, or "place without night"; it flourished to such a degree that by 1780, the number of prostitutes exceeded four thousand, and would grow to over seven thousand by the end of the Edo period in 1868.

To the consternation of the ruling elite, the pleasure quarters acted as social levelers, with clients drawn from the samurai ranks of the *yamanote* as well as the merchants and tradespeople of the *shitamachi*. The only requirement for entry was the admission fee. And there were services to accommodate every purse. Aside from the houses for licentious pleasure, there were drinking establishments, restaurants, and shops near the entrance that sold *amigasa*, broad-brimmed hats made from straw that could be purchased by customers such as samurai and priests, who preferred their identities to go unnoticed. The absence of behavioral parameters in the pleasure quarters, and the abandonment of the strict social codes that determined class relations, was a matter of increasing concern to the authorities.

The services of the *jiroro*, the lowest-ranking purveyors of pleasure in the hierarchy of the flesh trade, were swift and without the pretentions of affection; those of the more celestial *tayu*, high-ranking courtesans, were more lingering and nuanced. Adept at witty repartee and double entendres, *tayu* were accomplished at flower-arranging, incense-differentiation, sake-pouring, singing, dancing, haiku composition, fortune-telling, and the playing of the shamisen. The pleasures of the flesh, like the administration of a strong potion, were the final ecstasy that would guarantee the return of a patron, even if it ruined him.

Exalted symbols of beauty, the *tayu* were sumptuously robed, the outer lineaments of their kimonos stiff with gold thread; safflower juice was used to make the rouge they applied to their lips. Teeth-blackening was common; the powder used for this was made from a mixture of iron filings and nails soaked in tea and sake. A striking fashion at one time was to paint the lower lip with a gloss of iridescent green rouge. With faces, necks, and hands luminous with the otherworldly effects of white cosmetics, the *tayu* resembled painted icons, effigies whose power was, arguably, more voluptuous than spiritual. The novelist Shozan wrote, "The dress of the *tayu* is a long robe made of luxuriously embroidered silk brocade. Her head is ornamented with a brilliance of tortoise-shell hairpins that radiate around her like the aureole of a saint." The satirist Ihara Saikaku sounded a more cautionary note when he observed, "The clothing of the courtesan is so arranged that her red crepe de chine undergarment will open to reveal a glimpse of white ankle, or even the thigh. When men see such a vision, they become insane, lavishing even money entrusted to them." The *tayu*, emblems of a divine but costly beauty, would eventually cultivate themselves out of existence.

Women like the *tayu*, who could comfortably afford such costly adjuncts to their profession and lifestyle, kept a number of adult toys in their closets, presumably both for self-pleasure during slack times and for the benefit of customers. A dried sea cucumber—tube-shaped, with nobbly outer layers—was filled with water to serve as an embellished dildo. Other dildos were uniform in shape, but their proportions varied from giant decorative versions to tiny "finger" varieties. There was a brisk trade in aphrodisiacs, though they were costly. Korean and Chinese ginseng roots were mixed with pulverized rhinoceros horn and wild herbs that could be found along the banks of the Sumida River to make extracts and potions. These were quite expensive, and the *tayu* were virtually the only people who could procure them.

Economics were an equally important consideration for both patrons and procurers of women. The influx of men working at the newly built warehouses and lumberyards of Fukagawa, east of the river, created the need—in a city outside the jurisdiction of Edo magistrates where males vastly outnumbered women—for an unlicensed pleasure quarter that was more affordable than the Yoshiwara. The establishment of a temple and shrine in the area stimulated commerce, and soon there were shops and teahouses staffed by young women. Many of the lower-ranking prostitutes were on display along the back streets of the quarter, where they could be seen sitting behind latticework windows.

A similar level of service, catering to those of more slender means, existed at Shinjuku, the first westward stop of the Koshu Kaido—the post road running westward from Edo toward Nagano and the Japan Sea. The rough-and-ready temporary inns set up in 1698 as lodgings for travelers were shut down in 1718 because of an incident involving a customer and a "rice-serving girl" at one of the many brothels catering to their guests. It would be almost fifty years before the Shinjuku post town was reopened, but it went on to become one of the foremost of Edo's six licensed quarters.

When it came to illness and death—the great levelers—there was not a great deal to distinguish the low-ranking *sancha* or *jijoro* prostitutes in quarters like Shinjuku from the courtesans of the Yoshiwara, known for cultivating a theatrical indolence and arrogance. Women from both the highest ranks of the Yoshiwara and the less-exalted pleasure quarters were bedeviled by sexually transmitted diseases; most of the lower-ranking women died in their early twenties, and were mourned by few. At Jokan-ji temple in Minowa, a working-class district of northeast Tokyo, the remains of more than eleven thousand young women who perished while working in the pleasure quarters of the city during the Edo era are buried in a common, unmarked grave. Brothel staff would dump the bodies over the temple wall, giving rise to the establishment's better-known name, Nagekomi-dera (the Waste-disposal Temple). A belief that prostitutes would return to haunt a person who treated their body with disrespect ensured that the corpses were wrapped in straw before being dropped over the wall, although this was the identical custom observed for dead animals.

Aside from their purely carnal functions, the pleasure quarters and their easily disposed and replenished women provided more than the playhouses themselves. Playwrights, artists, and poets found boundless subjects in the pleasure quarters. Far from being a public seraglio with sex as the dominant theme, the Yoshiwara in particular became the center of an alternative culture marked by a decadent aestheticism and connoisseurship of taste that were depicted by some of the greatest artists of the city. The quarter gave birth to fashions in dress, and its speech mannerisms and styles of deportment were widely emulated.

As subjects, the pleasure quarters were assiduously avoided by the older schools of painters, despite the fact that they existed not only for the sake of sexual gratification, but also as cultural seedbeds that would overwhelm the arts patronized by the aristocracy. Representations of urban styles in the pleasure quarters and elsewhere were derisively compared to the refinements of the Tosa and Kano schools of painting. It was not until the appearance of Moronobu Hishikawa, one of the early practitioners of ukiyo-e, that more refined commercially available woodblock print images began to emerge. Moronobu established a reputation for executing *Yoshiwara no tei* (Scenes from the Yoshiwara) and work in other erotic print genres.

Moronobu's early prints were monochrome, but it was not long before pigments were added, resulting in the vibrant *nishiki-e* or "brocade prints" of artists like Suzuki Harunobu. In *Pictures of Japanese Occupations*, Moronobu, drawn to the exuberant complexity of Edo street life, created a highly realistic visual document of the working habits of ordinary townspeople—its tradesmen and fishmongers; peddlers of clams, rice cakes, and bean curd; washerwomen; salt-gatherers and priests; apothecaries and harlots.

Kabuki actors, with their sumptuous costumes, wigs, and extravagant makeup, made wonderful print subjects. The word *kabuki* had connotations of sexual license, and by the early seventeenth century it was synonymous with being out of the mainstream. Much beloved of the pleasure-seeking townspeople, *kabukimono* were male popinjays who sallied around the city in flamboyant dress, offending none but the authorities. Because the early female Kabuki troupes were associated with prostitution, it was ordained that women's roles would be played by young men. In Edo, a city fixated on the erotic, this merely created another problem, as quarrels over the favors of attractive young actors broke out among members of the Buddhist priesthood and samurai in the audiences. Henceforth, female parts were to be acted only by older adult males.

Edo's first licensed Kabuki theater was founded at Nakabashi in 1624, but because of its proximity to the castle, it was relocated to Negicho (now known as Ningyocho), and then moved once again to Sakaicho. By 1714, there were three major theaters in the area: Ichimura-za, Morita-za and Nakamura-za. The auditoriums were dark, with stages lit by candles; black-hooded stagehands moved through the shadows, unnoticed by audiences. Where special effects were needed to heighten the drama or for performances of ghost stories, trap doors could be used for sudden visitations. Small boys illuminated the ghastly visages of actors by holding lit candles beneath their faces. The overpowering smells of wax, camellia hair oil, women's face powder, and clouds of tobacco smoke, combined with the tight seating arrangements, must have made for a suffocating theater experience, especially in the summer months, when there was little or no ventilation in the theaters.

Ichikawa Danjuro was the leading actor of the Genroku era (1688–1703). An exponent of the bravura *aragoto* or "rough" heroic style of Kabuki, embodying the superhuman features and valor of the heroes he played, Danjuro's highly charged, masculine performances were enriched with patterned kimonos, scarlet silk underwear, and dazzling red-and-white makeup. Such was the legacy of Danjuro that he remains a tutelary deity among actors even today.

Book-publishing flourished at this time, as paper costs had

fallen and literacy levels were on the rise. With the appearance of booksellers around 1650, public demand grew for picture books, scholarly works on Confucianism and moral conduct, travel journals and diaries, and works of literature. There was also great demand for light narratives, music manuscripts, comic verse, woodblock prints of the pleasure quarters and guides to the same, and anatomical treatises on "Dutch learning." The latter were of great interest to physicians eager to learn about advances in Western medicine and surgery. If you could not afford to buy a title in one of Edo's well-stocked bookstores, there were itinerant peddlers who carried their wares on their backs, renting them out for five days at a time in exchange for a small fee. By the late 1830s, the number of book lenders in Edo exceeded 800. Little wonder that literacy levels in Edo ranked among the highest in the world at that time.

Writing could get you into serious trouble, though, especially if you had the temerity to lampoon the authorities. Reactionary policies and edicts like the Kansei reforms in the late eighteenth century typically involved the promulgation of new censorship laws and an effort to dissuade the warrior class from dabbling in writing fiction.

A surge in literary activity and the cultural refinement it represented was embodied in the person of the great haiku poet Matsuo Basho. In the winter of 1680, a disciple of the writer built a humble reed-thatched cottage for him on the eastern shores of the Sumida River. Erected on land owned by Sugiyama Sampu, a wealthy lumber merchant, it was exposed to sea winds from the bay, typhoons, and the constant threat of tsunami. Fukugawa was by then a semi-rural area built on reclaimed delta land. As there were no natural springs or aquifers, water was delivered by boat. The poet had taken his pen name from the gift of a *basho* (banana) tree given by a student. The leaves appealed to Basho's aesthetic of rustic simplicity, recalling, as he said, the "injured tail of a phoenix. When they are torn, they remind me of a green fan ripped by the wind." Furthermore, pointing out that the *basho* had no value as timber, he added, "I admire the tree for its very uselessness." The master named his cottage the Basho-an.

It was an accepted fact for Edo citizens that everything could be lost in a moment. The huge firestorm that devoured Basho's neighborhood on December 28, 1682, left him homeless; he saved his own life by jumping into the river and hiding under a reed mat.

The satisfaction he enjoyed from the recognition of his work was not always matched by material comfort. As the poet wrote one cold night:

> An oar striking waves
> The sound freezing my bowels
> Evening tears

In an age of almost excessive refinement, of mannerism in dress, taste and language, the nuances and symbolism of verse were implicitly understood. In the summer of 1676, pressed for funds, Basho wrote:

> Placed on a fan
> Wind from Mount Fuji
> A gift from Edo

The imagery would have been immediately apparent to the more urbane reader. It is considered a gesture of immense elegance to offer a present on a fan instead of sullying it with the bare hand; thus, the impecunious Basho is offering the coolness of the fan itself as a gift to his host.

In Basho's day, Edo's complex network of rivers, canals, and moats were the equal of roads. Water stood for more than just a commercial conduit, being the medium for a floating social life. In the highly structured class system of Edo, the banks, water, and *hirokoji* ("open spaces") adjacent to the Sumida River and other public congregation points came to represent areas of greater permissible freedom. The superimposition of the river upon the life of the city was an ordinary process whose natural energy matched the vitality of Edo. If it was a city of water, it was probably closer to Suzhou than Venice, with plenty of the former's storehouses, granaries, and quays and none of the latter's palazzi or monuments to great wealth.

The Sumida served in the way that all rivers should, by bringing nature into the city. The oars of pilots plying the river were still apt to become entangled in waterweeds; beautiful white birds, oyster-catchers known as *miyakodori* (capital birds), could still be seen in the waters of the river into the early years of the twentieth century. Cranes were a common sight, their presence during the migratory season adding grace notes to the riverbanks of Edo, though shoguns had taken to hunting them with falcons during the winter, taking excursion parties to Mikawashima, an area to the northwest of Shin-Yoshiwara.

The presence and well-being of animals took on particular significance during the tenure of the shogun Tsunayoshi, (1680–1709), whose birth year happened to be the Year of the Dog. An influential priest in the service of his mother persuaded the impressionable young man to forbid the killing and mistreatment of dogs and other animals under penalty of death. Tsunayoshi accordingly issued his "Edicts on Compassion for Living Things," and ordered compounds to be built in Edo to accommodate stray dogs. The number of canines in Edo rose sharply, their nocturnal barking and fighting depriving residents of their sleep. Animal-rights ordinances were issued nationwide, but only appear to have been enforced in Edo; people were tried and sentenced in a total of sixty-nine cases, and thirteen of them were executed. Edo citizens were required to address dogs using the form *O-inu sama* (Honorable Mr. Dog). The edicts were immediately abrogated by Tsunayoshi's successor, the shogun Ienobu. A revenge of sorts was posthumously visited upon Tsunayoshi by the good people of Edo, who would forever refer to him by the title *inu-kubo*, the "Dog Shogun."

The dispensation of favors by Tsunayoshi, much resented by the people of Edo, appeared to have been predicated on the shogun's ever-changing sexual predilections, which were mostly centered on males. The *Sanno Gaiki*, a historical document, is quite clear on the topic: "The shogun preferred sex with males of all social rankings, providing they were handsome." The record lists 130 appointments of this kind. Tsunayoshi was not a physically imposing man: life-sized Buddhist mortuary tablets kept at Daiju-ji temple in Okazaki city in Aichi prefecture record his height at 124 centimeters (4 feet).

Mercifully for the protein-deficient people of Edo, fish were not listed among Tsunayoshi's creatures deserving of compassion. A large fish market operated at Shiba, along the bay to the southeast of the fort. A general market just outside the castle gates called Yokkaichi (Fourth-Day Market) sold dried and salted fish brought down the coast from the Kamakura area.

Edo's largest rice granaries were located in Kuramae, where berths cut into the riverbanks housed the tributary rice shipped from the domains to the shogun's own storehouses. Rice brokers were able to amass great wealth. The rice merchants were known for their profligacy, squandering much of their wealth in the licensed quarters of Yoshiwara and Yanagibashi. Meat was not commonly consumed, due in part to the Buddhist proscription on the eating of animal flesh. Meat was consumed as a "medicinal food," however; some believed that it was an elixir. Animal flesh, referred to as "mountain whale," could be bought at hunters' markets like the one in Yotsuya, or at butcher's shops in the vicinity of Komadome Bridge, where deer, wild boar, monkey, and varieties of game were sold.

Other creatures, on the other hand, were not consumed, but given supernatural forms and persona. Little-understood geological occurrences like earthquakes were blamed on an outlandishly sized earth spider; in the later years of Edo, seismic activity was attributed to a giant catfish that caused tremors when it became disgruntled and thrashed its tail. In a world where supernatural forces and divination were inseparable from quotidian life, natural disasters were interpreted as a form of divine retribution.

Major earthquakes and fires, a common combination, occurred in 1694 and 1703. A year later, flooding was followed by outbreaks of cholera, plague, and measles. Intense tremors shook Edo on October 4, 1707, as Mount Fuji belched ash over the city. Two days later, the mountain erupted, the fire and lava from its cone turning the sky above Edo a deep red. With ash and hot cinders falling on the city and turning daytime into night, people took to carrying lanterns. Others doused hessian cloth with water and wrapped it around their heads as a precaution against falling cinders. As people crowded into temples and shrines to offer prayer for divine intercession, the eruption was inevitably attributed to failings in governance, corruption, and political malfeasance.

Evacuating people from the impoverished warren of the *shitamachi* was almost impossible. The sheer number of inhabitants itself was a barrier to escape. Ieyasu had encouraged the immigration of merchants, fishermen, manufacturers, and craftspeople to his new military bastion so they could service the needs of the court and the nobility and their retainers. The population of Edo was half a million by 1630, and at the end of the century it had doubled, making Edo the most populous city in the world. The world at large, however, was hardly aware of Edo, and had yet to discover its extraordinary material growth and cultural efflorescence.

A rare survivor of war and disaster, the magnificent Toshogu in Ueno Park is one of Japan's designated Cultural Properties. (Photo by Joe Mabel, printed under the Creative Commons 2.0 Attribution-Share Alike 2.0 Generic and 3.0 Attribution-Share Alike 3.0 Unported Licenses)

CHAPTER 2

The Restive City

*Flowering of culture – Neo-Confucianism – A rising
merchant class – The green city – Perry's black ships
– Assassinations, war, turmoil – The end of Edo*

On an unseasonably snowy morning in January 30, 1703, an event took place that electrified Edo, plunging it into a protracted debate about honor, duty, and punishment. Lord Kira Yoshinaga, a daimyo whose sumptuous estate lay close to the Sumida River in Ryogoku, had been appointed to instruct young Lord Asano Naganori Takuminokami in the finer points of court ritual. Failing to receive the gifts he felt entitled to and openly derisive of his charge, Lord Kira goaded Asano to the point where he drew his dagger and struck out at the older man—a grievous offence at court that was punishable by death. The assailant was arrested and ordered to commit *seppuku*, ritual self-disembowelment.

With the Asano family disinherited and its estates divided up, its retainers became masterless *ronin* ("wave men"). Oishi Kuranosuke, Asano's elder councilor, began secretly plotting his master's revenge along with forty-six other former Asano retainers. Cognizant that Kira's men would be keeping them under strict surveillance, the *ronin* set about obliterating any traces of samurai bearing in their public demeanor, blending in with the populace by taking up the activities of petty merchants, laborers, carpenters, peddlers, and tinkers. Oishi himself repaired to Kyoto, where he adopted a life of drunkenness and dissipation, going as far as to evict his wife and two young children from his home and take up with a young concubine of ill repute. Oishi's debauchery and apparent desire for self-annihilation were dutifully reported to Kira, who began to lower his guard. It was an effective ruse.

Asano's former retainers saw their imminent act less as revenge than high ritual. Accordingly, they dressed in new clothing, donning white underwear of padded silk, *hakama* trousers, black padded kimonos bearing family crests, gauntlets, leggings, and black-and-white hoods and mantles. Some followed the ancient custom of burning incense in their helmets. If the enemy cut their heads off, their helmets would be fragrantly scented.

In the early morning hours of January 30, 1703, Oishi's men stormed Kira's snowbound villa. Several of Kira's men fought to the last, while others, including his son, dropped their weapons and fled. The *ronin* found Kira's bed still warm, but empty. A brief search of the property revealed an old hut used to store charcoal, and it was there they found their prey. The identity of the man in the hut, who was dressed in a white satin sleeping-gown, was confirmed by the scar from Asano's dagger. Offered the chance to commit seppuku, Kira refused. Oishi then stepped forward and beheaded him with Lord Asano's own sword.

After walking through streets covered in an unusually thick layer of snow, carrying the head in a bucket, the *ronin* boarded a ferry that took them to the pine-covered shore beneath Sengaku-ji temple. They washed the head in a well, and then placed it before Asano's tomb. Each retainer kneeled, and, burning a pinch of incense, prayed for his master's repose. After this ritual, the abbot of the temple invited them into the main hall where he served them a temple breakfast of simple rice gruel.

The retainers had dispensed justice in perfect accordance with the code of honor demanded by samurai ethics, so how could the shogunate enact its own? Scholars were employed by the authorities to write briefs examining the moral and penal issues. The only conceivable judgment one that would save face for all parties was the eventual order issued to the *ronin* to commit suicide. The self-disembowelments of the forty-seven retainers, who ranged in age from fifteen to seventy-seven, took place on February 4, 1703. The event quickly passed into popular culture, with woodblock prints portraying scenes from the revenge tale, and a major Kabuki play, *Chushingura* (Treasury of Loyal Retainers), was written by the great playwright Chikamatsu Monzaemon. Theatrical representations of the incident were invariably set in the past, however, to comply with government prohibitions on portraying recent events.

Ronin more fractious than the disciplined assassins who dispatched Lord Kira roamed the streets of Edo. Cast out of service for misdemeanors, or made redundant by disgraced masters stripped of their privileges, these men behaved unpredictably, posing political problems for the shogunate, as they often became involved in brawls and riots. In the 1790s, the shogun's chief councilor, Matsudaira Sadanobu, had a detention center built on Tsukudajima, an artificial island in the Sumida River, where *ronin*, along with vagrants, could be held while they learnt a trade. It was a solution of sorts, though a scheme to turn men trained as warriors into harmless artisans was an imperfect one.

Economically bled by the *sankin kotai* system of rotating residence, the warrior class became more effete as they devoted their time less to martial arts and more to the pleasures of patronizing Noh plays, holding incense parties, collecting fine pieces of ceramic ware, and attending the tea ceremony. Groups of low-ranking *hatamoto* (bannermen), though officially the shogun's fighting force, often found themselves with time on their hands. These young samurai, with their notoriously low stipends, could be troublesome in their idle moments. They refused to settle their debts when cash-strapped, and could be socially disruptive, even violent, when flush with money. The notorious Shiratsuka-Gumi, or "White Hilt Gang," typified the brash, unstable elements that would become a feature of Edo street life, emerging in the early 1640s only to be eliminated by the authorities at the end of the seventeenth century. The gang's name came from the swords they carried, which were conspicuously longer than normal and decorated, like their obi (sashes), with showy white fittings. They took their sartorial rebellion and contempt for convention to new heights by wearing long kimonos in summer and short ones in winter. To promote an affected swagger, they placed lead at the bottom of their kimono hems, causing their clothes to swing.

It was a showy form of representation that had something in common with the urban, or at least etymological, origins of Kabuki. The original meaning of the word *kabuki*—from the verb *kabuku*, which carried the sense of leaning or tilting off-balance—had little or no connection to a theatrical form. It also suggested the idea of having an eccentric personal appearance, and acting in a free-spirited, uninhibited manner. By the seventeenth century, it had acquired the meaning of "being unusual or out of the ordinary," and also connoted sexual debauchery. The image of the *kabukimono*—the rowdy, swaggering young blades of Edo—embodies some of the spirit and style of the age. The subversive reputation of Kabuki, an egalitarian art affordable to all but the poorest, and widely supported by the lower orders of Edo society—and its transgressive potential—evident in its frequent breaking of sumptuary laws and tendency to draw its subject matter from current, often sensitive events—never failed to exacerbate the authorities. The Tokugawa authorities, despising all forms of plebeian theater, were never completely able to cut the townspeople off from a drama they had adopted as their own. Kabuki would eventually have to compete for audiences with *yose* (variety halls). An affordable alternative to the bathhouses and meaner bordellos of the Yoshiwara, *yose* provided the townspeople with a lively program of comedians, jugglers, dancers and storytellers.

Crossings close to main streets and bridges were requisitioned as open entertainment spaces called *hirokoji*. Here, social ranking tended to blur as visitors' attention was distracted by top spinners, acrobatics, magic shows, side stalls, tooth-powder vendors, and displays of exotic creatures—camels, Bengali oxen, ostriches, cassowaries, and donkeys—brought into the country by Dutch traders in Nagasaki. Quite how many of these animals, often presented as official gifts to shoguns, ended up in the *hirokoji* of Edo, is unclear. Performances of "beggar's Kabuki" by minor troupes were held in makeshift theaters made from reed mats. Actors doubled up on roles, each side of their face made up to represent a different character. The two sides of their bodies were likewise dressed in the costume of each respective protagonist. More circus-like acts involved performers leaping through baskets spiked with sword blades and rattan hoops affixed with burning candles.

The most popular of the Edo *hirokoji* was at the western approach to the Ryogoku Bridge spanning the Sumida River. Inevitably, the unscrupulous preyed on the crowds: mountebanks sold snake medicine and miracle formulas to the credulous; Buddhist exorcisms were as popular as lantern shows and performances by illusionists.

The firebreak at Ueno, at the southeast corner of Shinobazu Pond in Shitaya, provided a similar fare of acrobats, fire-eaters, dancers, preachers, and sermonizers. The lanes behind its teahouses, stalls, and booths offered the services of *kekoro*, low-class prostitutes working in the district's cramped brothels.

Like its Ryogoku counterpart, Ueno offered makeshift tents, stalls, and booths made of reed and wattle set up for performances by acrobats, jugglers, and storytellers. Inside the tents you could see peep shows; exhibitions of human freaks; lifelike models of goblins, giants and Dutch galleons; and crude pornographic shows. There were *tableaux vivants* of a similar voyeuristic nature, featuring realistic models of courtesans in various stages of undress.

Okuyama, a patch of land behind the main hall of Senso-ji temple, was just as animated. There were brothels posing as archery galleries, conjurers, and automata; displays of papier-mâché figures depicted red-haired barbarians, scenes from Kabuki, and a particularly terrifying model of the old hag of Adachi Moor, a bloodthirsty woman who enticed travelers into her hut in order to rob and murder them. There were stalls dispensing sake and tea, and others where you could find cosmetics, hairpins, boxwood combs, plants, medicines, and solutions for blackening teeth.

Edo was a bodacious, pullulating city, one whose population by 1720 exceeded 1.3 million, making it the largest city in the world. London, the most congested city in Europe, had a population of 850,000 by 1801, Beijing roughly one million. Any notion of a city boundary had long vanished. Because of the nature of employment in Edo, where trades and crafts largely excluded women, only a third of its population was female. By 1720, there was population parity between the *shitamachi* and the *yamanote*; each had roughly 650,000 inhabitants. The disproportion, however, was in density, as the *shitamachi* region covered a mere 16 percent of the surface area of Edo.

Governance and infrastructure initiatives may have originated from an elite, demographically small class, but it was Edo's own inhabitants—the lower orders—who seem to have dictated the character of the city. Those with three generations of uninterrupted Edo ancestry could now lay claim to the moniker "Edokko," meaning "true child of Edo." Edokko prided themselves on being unproductive and expressed open contempt for pecuniary concerns; their sense of identity could be heard in expressions like "The true Edokko loves fires and brawls," and "It's an unqualified Edokko who hoards money." Rather than creating a sense of grievance and separateness, the impoverished living conditions east of the river inspired a fierce, confrontational pride in the inhabitants. They were not universally liked. The diligent tradesmen of Osaka, for example, derided the Edokko as "rakes and profligates of Edo, hot-bloodied but hairy-brained, putting assets into bottomless bags." The Edokko embodied the energy and appetite of the city, representing a powerful, potentially untamed force that was, accordingly, the object of much suspicion by the authorities. The townspeople were not exactly manning the barricades, but there were subtle forms of subversion taking place. The backers of this process were the wealthier merchant families that supported popular culture in all its prolific forms—from the red chambers of the pleasure quarters to Kabuki, to fashions in dress, to new work from members of the literati and woodblock artists.

A slew of gifted writers and satirists with a good eye for social follies, excesses, and injustice aided social change. Edo offered freedoms not vouchsafed for in other major cities like Osaka and Kyoto. It was possible for people not listed on the Census Register, for example, to pass unnoticed in Edo's rich social mix, making a living as day laborers. It was relatively easy to blend in with the social outcasts and criminal class.

Inhabiting the lower rungs of the social ladder did not exclude the townspeople from developing an urbane, codified style of manners and tastes. A bravura aesthetic involving a loud flair, ostentation, and straightforwardness flourished in Edo. A more subdued and understated style was closely associated with the wealthy Low City merchant, who had connections with the Yoshiwara. The acquisition of such tastes represented a greater degree of cultural discernment. The more rebellious, lower-class practitioners of a brasher, more vivid form of style and taste, on the other hand, preferred districts like Fukagawa, a working-class pleasure quarter that flourished in the early decades of the nineteenth century. The former were likely to engage in amorous dalliances in the cultural setting of literature, witty conversation, art, and music; the latter to pursue simpler, more easily attainable forms of desire. In this period of ripe, ultimately subversive culture, the Buddhist term *ukiyo*, denoting the impermanence of life, was appropriated and repurposed to express the "floating" decadence and social flux of the era.

In order to regulate populist sentiments and tendencies aimed at engendering social freedoms, authority requires a higher order of moral legitimacy than the common penal system can provide. When power is absolutist rather than founded on consent, it seeks justification in writ, religion, legacy, or history. The Edokko and their class stood at the opposite end of the social spectrum to the ruling class, whose adopted code of Neo-Confucianism, with its doctrine of subjugation to a male hierarchy whose ultimate model was the state, suited the government's aim of instilling an ironclad loyalty toward authority.

The original tenets of Confucianism were reinterpreted by Hayashi Razan (1583–1687), a scholar of the classics who set about excising the more philosophical or metaphysical aspects of the original Chinese tradition while emphasizing ethics and a theory of governance based on a system of obedience that would become an exclusively state creed. Under this system, the young were raised to fulfill their duties to the state, not to seek their fortunes or improve themselves. Lectures at the highest scholarly institute, the Shoheizaka Institute of Learning in Yushima, focused on a doctrine that became known as Tokugawa Confucianism. Its deliberate intrusiveness even dictated the way people were obliged to dress. Citizens of high rank were allowed to dress in resplendent colors, while those of the lower orders were expected to choose muted tones that would promote their invisibility. The resourceful merchant classes, with increasing amounts of cash at their disposal, were able to bend these strict sartorial rules.

The continuing fires that plagued Edo, however, were not so easily addressed. When conflagrations occurred, they could spread rapidly. Residents might become agitated if they noticed a change in the behavior of the white smoke rising from the fires of public bathhouses, as the winds from the mountains of Chichibu (a region northwest of Edo) blew down on the city. The bridge at Nihonbashi was destroyed by fire yet again in 1806; hundreds of townspeople fled from a fire at the nearby Echigoya warehouse.

It is ironic that Edo, a city interpenetrated by so much water, exploded into flames so frequently, but the water could be a problem, too. If you lived near rivers or canals, you enjoyed good transportation, fresh fish, and the delight of water-cooled air during the stifling summer months. You could also suffer from inundations: Large areas of Edo were built on low reclaimed land, so flooding was an ever-present risk. In the year 1742 alone, some 4,000 people perished in storms and floods. Typhoons and high tides combined in 1791 to wipe out the entire entertainment district of Susaki, a pleasure quarter located east of the Sumida River in flood-prone Fukagawa. A massive tidal wave swept through Fukagawa in 1854, destroying all but a few of its fragile weatherboard homes.

Livelihoods and trade in many districts were nourished by water. Fukagawa depended on the uninterrupted operation of its waterways, as it was an important warehouse and wholesale center for oil, salt, sake, beans, fertilizer, and other commodities that had to be moved. Its wharves were also busy loading timber from merchants who operated in the adjacent district of Kiba. The celebration of the Suijin Sai (Festival of the River God) took place at the Sumidagawa Shrine at the end of May on the east bank of the river. On or after this date a great fireworks display was held on the river. Known as the *kawa-biraki*, or "river-opening," the original intent of the fireworks, when the magnificent displays were first held in the early eighteenth century, was to cleanse the city of cholera.

While writers like Napo Ota were able to exercise a degree of latitude in recording the disagreeable realities of life in Edo, there was no Edo equivalent of the eighteenth-century English painter, social critic, and satirist William Hogarth, with his depictions of gin addicts, streetwalkers, child scavengers, dissipated aristocrats, and the idle and loutish. Neither was there any parallel to the depictions of common laborers seen in the illustrations of the Victorian artist George Scarf. What we do have as examples of city documentation are woodblock prints and the increasingly more outspoken pages of popular novels, satirical verse known as *senryu*, and events on the stage. Edo had become a notably literate city. Visual literacy was already highly refined, but with a boom in publishing, all manner of reading became available. Followers of neo-Confucianism could pick up a copy of the *Kogiroku* (Record of Filial Piety and Ethical Righteousness), while brushing shoulders in the same bookstore with readers hungry for *kibyoshi*, adult comic books written mostly in the simple hiragana syllabary.

The lethargy that defined the class- and privilege-obsessed samurai sprang partly from their contempt for trade and commerce. Stringent sumptuary laws and edicts were introduced with the intention of forcing commoners back into their allotted positions in the social order. All this achieved was to reduce the display of conspicuous affluence among the merchant class. Forbidden to wear vibrant colors and silk, the outward attire of the merchant class became sober, but silken fabrics of the highest quality were sewn into the underside of their modest cotton apparel. Prohibited from living in two-floor homes, they had carpenters make mezzanine units for them. The government even went so far as to prohibit commoners from using silver leaf and gold lacquer as decorative touches, and from owning such luxuries as tortoiseshell hairpins, cosmetic boxes, combs, and finer varieties of eating utensils. These restrictions were largely ignored by a populace that understood how difficult it was to enforce them. Such minor examples of subversion were impossible to control in a system showing increasing signs of decay. A conspiratorial irony was maintained in order for the authorities to keep face: the ruling class would pretend they were affluent; the merchant class would affect an appearance of penury.

Hairline cracks in the system were already evident in the undermining of the social hierarchy. By the middle of the eighteenth century, many of the social strictures, including the segregation of classes, were honored more in the breach. Once-unthinkable instances of impoverished samurai marrying the daughters of wealthy merchant families were not uncommon. Oppressive legislation like the Tenpo Reforms of 1841–43, which resulted in the arrest of leading writers, reformists, and liberal political figures, were frequently reissued, suggesting compliance was no easy matter. A popular saying at the time, in fact, was "The law lasts three days." It was becoming increasingly difficult to suppress information in the manner preferred by totalitarian states. Edo was rapidly conforming to Aristotle's definition of the ideal size of a city as one where news travels swiftly.

The city may have had fewer open spaces and public gardens than the cities of Europe or the New World, but flowers and greenery remained an important part of Edo life. Entranceways often featured a bonsai or potted tree, while the narrow borders of the house served to display morning glories, water plants, and calabashes. Compensating for the shortage of municipally planned and funded parks and gardens was the persistence of natural elements within the city and its boundaries. The semirural character of the cityscape was apparent to Englishman Sir Rutherford Alcock, who in the 1850s observed that Edo could "boast what no capital in Europe can—the most charming rides, beginning even in its center, and extending in every direction over wooded hills, through smiling valleys and shaded lanes, fringed with evergreens and magnificent timber." The summits of Edo's many northwestern slopes were blessed by clean gusts of air and commanding views. Alcock could ride over "undulating hills, high enough occasionally to give glimpses of the open country beyond," a pleasure that would be inconceivable today on these crowded, overdeveloped slopes. All manner of creatures—geese, cuckoos, foxes, badgers—thrived in Edo's natural environs. So clean were the rivers that boatmen drew water from them to brew their tea. Whitefish, Asakusa carp, roach, and bass were fished from boats, jetties, and earthen embankments along the Sumida River, where migrating red-crested cranes still waded.

The private gardens, teahouses, and temples of Mukojima, a region along the east bank of the river, enjoyed the patronage of some of the leading artists and writers of the day, including Tani Biuncho, Sakai Hoitsu, and the Confucian philosopher Kameda Hosai. A most charming congregation point was created in 1804 for these men of culture—all sons of Edo—at the Mukojima Hyakka-en garden. The refuge was created by Sahara Kiku, who sold his antique store and bought a plot of land near the river. With his friends, who were practicing artists and aspiring literati, Sahara set about making a garden whose flowers, plants, and herbs were associated with Japanese and Chinese literature. The stones that they inscribed with poems, aphorisms, and quotations can still be read. By the end of the century, however, Mukojima and its exquisite culture of taste would be transformed into an enjambment of temples, pilgrimage sites, and factories with billowing smokestacks. The cherry trees that lined its embankments were dying, the river and its aquatic life ruined by the spillage from coal barges.

Disfiguration and despoilment were imminent, but many of the old charms and graces still remained at the close of the Edo age. There were visible and audible distinctions between the city in the daytime and the nocturnal one. Knife-grinders, tobacco and pipe vendors, fortune-tellers, collectors of old clogs, strolling musicians, mendicant monks, water-bearers, coolies, pushers of handcarts, carpenters, porters, and apprentices worked along small lanes and alleys. In the daytime, temple bells, the lap of the ferryman's oars, the summer insects in the grand estate gardens or along the canals, and the stirring of air under the wings of riverside cranes augmented the sensations of living in Edo. At night it was a dark and silent city, its guardhouses, sentries, and watchmen protecting it not so much against foreign armies, but from the encroachment of time. All of this would be lost, drowned out by the din of a new, as-yet-inconceivable city that would soon take form.

Food was a consummate preoccupation for the people of Edo, as it is today. Refinement and connoisseurship in matters of food extended even to quite ordinary dishes. A simple bowl of soba buckwheat noodles topped with scallops and strips of roasted seaweed, for example, would be understood to resemble hailstones scattered across grass, a seasonal indicator of early spring. Food was not always plentiful. The periodic scarcity of basic food commodities, the alternation between feast and famine, could have dire results. When crops failed, people went hungry. A craving for food led inevitably to rice riots, with the poorer elements of Edo, the lower social strata with no surplus provisions, storming the rice granaries of wealthy merchants. In 1733, a dramatic hike in rice prices set off riots throughout the city. Rice depots like the granary and shop of Takama Denbei were looted in violent incidents that prefigured the larger "Tenmei riots" of 1787.

Rice shortages and famine followed the 1780 eruption of Mount Asama in Nagano, an event that forced thousands of peasants to flood into Edo. Starvation drove many vagrants and even Edo residents to take their own lives by drowning themselves in the Sumida River. The famished and embittered, accusing merchants of causing the food shortages by hoarding stock, formed mobs and stormed the city's granaries. Social disorder was barely averted with the distribution of an emergency stock of rice after a series of famines and a sudden outbreak of fires that took place during the Tenpo era (1830–44).

Despite these disturbances, the authorities remained confident that looting could be contained through better food provisioning, and that any stirrings of political opposition would be quite different from Europe, where Enlightenment values had turned thinking elites against autocracy, and where, in France, the citizenry had extracted a savage revenge against their leaders in the revolution of 1789. The ordinary Japanese citizen knew little, if anything, of these world-transforming events and popular movements.

Edo at this point in time was more likely defined by the currents of culture than seismic political developments, swayed more by its writers and artists than it was by its neo-Confucian masters or the increasing lassitude of the warrior class. In the woodblock prints of great artists like Hokusai and Hiroshige, even in the later days of Edo, we see a defiantly premodern city, an urban landscape where people wear traditional clothing and pursue crafts and professions that have changed little in centuries. There are no motorized or horse-drawn forms of transport. The wealthy are carried in palanquins; everybody else walks.

Unlike European artists, the men who depicted these scenes in vibrant prints rarely indulged in self-portraits. No images exist, for example, of the great artist and printmaker Hokusai Katsushika, but we imagine, even if he was not physically large, a great bear of a man, a force of life much given to pranks and publicity gimmicks. Given his sharp-tongued and cantankerous nature, it is a wonder he was never clamped in irons by the authorities waging a sporadic war on popular art and culture. He was a versatile artist who worked equally well with his left or right hand and painted with his fingernails, between his knees, or above his head.

At Gokoku-ji temple, in an early example of public performance art, Hokusai announced he was going to paint a huge picture of the figure Daruma using India ink and a giant brush made from reeds. A compulsive showman, he produced something even more daring for the shogun Ienari: a long sheet of paper covered in curving blue lines. He then daubed the feet of a live cockerel in red paint and chased it along the canvas, naming the finished work *Red Maples Along the Tatsuta River*.

You could be the most famous artist in the city and still not know where the next meal came from. To make ends meet, Hokusai also produced *shunga* ("spring pictures"), profitable pornographic prints intended largely for private viewing that also served as instructive visual manuals for young women about to celebrate their nuptials. One wonders if the images of men engaging in sex with supernatural creatures and monsters, images of Buddhist nuns impaling themselves on acolytes, the implausible scale of the tumescent phalluses, had the effect of stimulating or unnerving prospective brides. Hokusai created what is probably the single best-known image in the genre: a pearl-diving woman in ecstatic coitus with the tentacles of a writhing octopus.

As mores in the city eroded, more and more people lost themselves in depravity. The death in 1841 of the wretchedly debauched eleventh shogun, Ienari, who was said to have been serviced by no less than forty concubines, may have influenced the launch of the Tenpo Reforms of 1842.

Though difficult to enforce and ultimately counterproductive, the reforms represented an attempt to restore a feudal agricultural system. They were also an effort to hobble the growing economic power and cultural independence of the merchant and lower-class urban population, and to curb the rising power of popular culture, synonymous in the minds of Tokugawa rulers with a challenge to authority.

Fresh edicts were placed on displays of luxury and affluence, new sumptuary laws were announced, and parameters were set on theaters. The number of variety halls was reduced from more than five hundred to a mere fifteen. The authorities required the content of performances to be uplifting and edifying. The use of vivid colors for book covers was no longer permitted. Female hairdressers, musicians, and the owners of Asakusa's notorious archery stalls and galleries were deemed corrupting influences and banned. These measures were matched with censorship of ukiyo-e prints. Artists like the great Utagawa Kuniyoshi were prevented from producing illustrations of actors and courtesans, subjects that were among their best-selling works.

Artists circumvented restrictions by representing figures in different forms. In Utagawa's case, he anthropomorphized animals to stand in as courtesans and actors in works like *The Cat Actor's Expressions of Emotion* and *Entertainment Under an Unclear Moon*, the latter print representing, in feline form, women of the Yoshiwara pleasure district. The caricatures are not simply clever evasions, but broadsides at the ludicrousness of censorship. The works of artists like Utagawa were testimony to the vitality of a restive spirit, one that would soon overthrow the old order.

By the 1830s and 1840s the townspeople, acutely attuned to financial matters, could sense the faltering economic power of the Tokugawa family. Finding itself increasingly in debt to the merchant class, the regime debased the currency a staggering nineteen times between 1819 and 1837. The stipends handed out to samurai in the form of fixed quantities of rice had long fallen behind inflation. The government's attempt to reaffirm feudal control over what was now a sophisticated domestic economy conflicted with its own dependence on just such a system. Observing how the shogun had usurped power from emperors, the more literate samurai began questioning the inherent contradictions in the way the authorities interpreted the Confucian code of loyalty.

Under the policy of *sakoku*, a program of national isolation enforced in 1635, foreigners were excluded from entering Japan and Japanese from exiting it. The country may have been hermetically sealed from the rest of the world, but members of the shogunate were considerably better informed of developments in Asia than they were prepared to publicly acknowledge. They were well aware that Britain had occupied Singapore in 1819, defeated the Qing Empire in the First Opium War of 1839–42, acquired Hong Kong, and were well on the way—along with other European powers—to dominating Chinese trade, if not its politics. The better informed may have heard accounts of how British soldiers had desecrated the historic Summer Palace outside Beijing. As for the opium the British were flooding China with, the Tokugawas would have known this was not only a lucrative trading venture, but a systematic attempt to erode the physical health of the country. European nations were already demanding the establishment of settlements within Chinese ports like Tianshin. The British and French had become a dominant presence in Shanghai, a city the former had created from the mud flats of the Huangpu River estuary. Gun emplacements were built along Edo Bay in 1854, and a series of forts known as *odaiba* were put in place a little south of what is now Rainbow Bridge. The defenses, augmented with a large number of mock cannon, would have been woefully inadequate in the event of a military standoff against technologically superior Western forces.

July 8, 1853, saw the arrival of Commodore Matthew Calbraith Perry's *kurofune* ("black ships"), as the Japanese called the four American steam-powered vessels that sailed into Edo Bay. Perry's principal interest was trade, to open up Japanese ports to American ships; he had little interest in any kind of *mission civilisatrice*. In this respect he resembled the Dutch before him, who, as their main concerns were mercantile, assiduously avoided religious matters or domestic issues.

The Japanese, having been closed to the outside world since the reign of King James I, then abruptly exposed to it in the era of Queen Victoria, had never set eyes on a metal ship before, let alone one that could move forward without wind. Their awe was mixed with fear, which in turn was overcome through ostracism. In keeping with conventions of ukiyo-e, in which Westerners were depicted as *karasu-tengu*, or "crow goblins," one painting of Perry portrays him with demonic, glaring eyes and a menacingly long blue nose. Curiosity overcame fear when Perry and his men, eventually allowed ashore and flanked by the tallest and most muscular black bodyguards he could muster, carried to land a number of intriguing items, amounting to an exhibition or digest of Western technology. Among the objects set down on the sands were a telegraph machine, a sewing machine, a daguerreotype camera, and a steam-powered quarter-gauge model railroad. It was not long before a number of formerly inhibited samurai were climbing aboard the engine for joyrides along the beach. Unlike the crucifixes, icons, and plaster statues of the Virgin Mary that the Portuguese and Spanish had brought three centuries earlier, these were objects that could be put to good use.

For their part, the Japanese—armed with ancient muskets, swords, and halberds—presented lacquer boxes, teapots, porcelain bowls, and rich brocades and silks. Not to be outdone, perhaps, by the impressive bodyguards, the Japanese reception party brought out a number of sumo wrestlers. Perry was invited to land one of them a punch in the stomach. The agreement Perry signed with the shogunate after a second visit in 1854 gave America control of Japanese tariffs to all Western nations, and residency rights for foreigners.

The period from Perry's arrival in 1853 and the eventual overthrow of the government by anti-shogunal forces, a period known as the *bakumatsu* ("end of the shogunate") was a time of immense upheaval, violence, extremism, and instability. With foreign forces at the gates, an indecisive government in retreat, and uncertainty about the future abounding, the decade saw the advent of fierce but short-lived millenarian cults. Liberated by the prevailing instabilities, mobs congregated in Edo and other large cities, stirring hysteria by carrying Shinto images, cavorting half-naked in the streets, looting the homes of the wealthy, engaging in frenzied public sex and quasi-religious delirium, shouting out *"Ei—janai ka!"* (Why not? Who cares?).

An unannounced increase in the price of rice led to a predictable wave of riots across the city in 1866. Emergency stocks from the rice granaries in Asakusa were hastily distributed among the townspeople, but this time they failed to quell the riots, which turned into the semi-cultish "world renewal riots." Followers of these ideologies—which were also known as *yonaoshi*, or "reform the world" beliefs—were convinced that the prevailing upheavals presaged the birth of a new world, and aimed at nothing less than the overturning of the existing moral, political, and spiritual order. Efforts at suppression were like trying to close a steam vent; the natural energies of Edo citizens only intensified when suppressed. The women from the show tents set up at the eastern end of the Ryogoku Bridge, obscenely lifting their kimonos before rows of heavily armed samurai, represented a measure of the contemporary defiance towards authority.

Two powerful earthquakes in 1854 and 1855 were followed by downpours and flooding. In the unsanitary urban conditions, a deadly cholera epidemic broke out. The more ferocious of the two earthquakes, a magnitude 7.9 temblor, struck the city at 10 p.m. on November 11, 1855. Disaster often strikes the east of the city, and this was no exception: Some 4,000 citizens of the downtown *shitamachi* districts were killed and over 14,000 homes were lost. The fires that swept through the Yoshiwara pleasure quarter took the lives of many courtesans, prostitutes, and entertainers. Relentless downpours flooded large areas of the low-lying eastern districts of the city. The daimyo in the provinces sent in money and workers to reconstruct their residences in Edo, and were forced to rely on loans from merchants to make up for monetary shortfalls—an indicator of the influence exercised by this increasingly empowered class.

With more catastrophes expected, illegal catfish woodblock prints called *namazu-e* were printed and sold widely. One woodblock print made shortly after the disaster depicts a group of irate courtesans attacking the giant catfish that had purportedly caused the quake. At the rear of the scene is a group of stonemasons and carpenters rushing to rescue the beleaguered fish—a cynical commentary on the fact that earthquakes represented a windfall for artisans like these. There was money to be made in this climate of fear, and many unscrupulous vendors did just that, selling any number of invocations, charms, and prophetic and apotropaic devices to the gullible. Such talismans, however, failed to protect the citizens of Edo from another cholera epidemic that broke out in 1858.

Many of the adamantly superstitious people of Edo blamed their misfortunes on the arrival of Perry's black ships. Rumors and biased reports in broadsheets represented a tendency, still evident today, to blame the country's woes on outsiders. Foreigners, the visible embodiments of change—or pollution, according to some quarters—remained on their guard. Francis Hall, an American businessman, wrote in 1859 of starting out for a walk by "putting a revolver in one pocket and a copy of Tennyson in the other." The United States legation, under Townsend Harris, was opened in 1859 in Zenpuku-ji temple in Hiro-o. The mission came under attack by fanatic imperialist elements, who wished to restore the emperor to power and expel the Western "barbarians." The building was burnt to the ground and Harris's interpreter, the Dutchman Henry Heusken, murdered. Fourteen anti-Western swordsmen invaded the British legation in 1861, attacking its staff, wounding one attaché, and slashing the visiting British consul from Nagasaki across the forehead. The building was blown up two years later.

There were reports of some samurai who, fearing contamination by the modern, covered their heads with metal fans as they rode beneath newly installed telegraph wires. This was a little similar, perhaps, to what was happening in Shanghai, where some residents were complaining that the telegraph wires were interfering with the city's feng shui. The climate of violence was palpable.

On the morning of March 24, 1860, assassins opposed to any formal contact with the Western barbarians cut down Ii Naosuke, Lord of Hikone, and his guards as they were making their way through snow to the grounds of Edo Castle. Ii, a key advisor to the shogun, had—against the wishes of the emperor and his courtiers—signed the Unequal Treaties document with Western powers. The agreement, signed in 1858 between Japan, America, Britain, France, Russia, and the Netherlands, granted highly beneficial trading rights to foreign powers and forced Japan to open several ports to Western ships. Particularly irksome to the

Japanese was the inclusion in the document of a system of extra-territoriality that subjected foreign residents to the laws of their own consular courts. This meant the Japanese legal system was powerless to prosecute foreign criminal suspects.

Troops loyal to the Tokugawa shogun seized Edo Castle, but surrendered it to imperialist forces in 1868. The latter consisted largely of middle- and lower-ranking samurai from the western domains of Satsuma, Choshu, and Tosa who had enlisted the support of a number of court nobles and rural merchants opposed to the shogunate.

Although hostilities at Edo Castle were negotiated peacefully, no such resolution occurred on Ueno Hill when a hardcore group of shogunal forces known as the Shogitai, some two thousand in all, rallied for a final stand against soldiers pledging loyalty to the emperor. Hopelessly outnumbered, surrounded on all sides, and targeted by modern artillery, the rout of the Tokugawa loyalists was a slaughter, staining red the water of Shinobazu Pond and the dirt road in front of the Kuromon (Black Gate) where the worst fighting took place.

The superb buildings of Kan'ei-ji temple were a final casualty of the fighting. Symbols of Tokugawa authority, they were unceremoniously torched without a trace of consideration for their beauty. One building that escaped the flames was the magnificent Toshogu, a shrine honoring—of all things—the memory of Ieyasu, the first of the Tokugawa shoguns.

The late Edo era was a time of extraordinary cultural achievement, but repressive anachronisms undermined its survival, hindering its transition into the modern age. When anti-Tokugawa forces joined arms to destroy the regime that had ruled Japan for over 250 years, however, it was a restoration of imperial rule they sought, not a revolution.

This detailed replica of Ryounkaku, the "Cloud-Surpassing Pavilion," is an exhibit at the Edo-Tokyo Museum. Ryounkaku was a center of shopping, exhibitions and performances from its completion in 1890 until ravaged by the Great Kanto Earthquake (see page 10 of color insert). (Photo by Gryffindor, printed under the Creative Commons Attribution-Share Alike 3.0 Unported License).

CHAPTER 3

The Great Meiji Bazaar

A new order – Western-style architecture – New forms of entertainment – Industrialization – Rising nationalism

Upon Emperor Komei's death by smallpox, his fifteen-year-old son Mutsuhito was elevated to the throne on January 9, 1867. Algernon Mitford recorded his impressions after being present at a meeting between the emperor and the British minister to Japan, Sir Harry Parkes. According to Mitford, the new emperor, at five feet seven inches, was an unusually tall youth, with clear eyes and complexion and a naturally dignified demeanor.

If the ancient feudal order was about to be swept away, it still clung to the vestments of the monarch, who appeared before the British guests "in a white coat with padded long trousers of crimson silk trailing like a lady's court-train." Beneath a hat of black gauze, the young man's eyebrows were shaved, with substitutes painted high on his forehead; "his cheeks were rouged and his lips painted with red and gold." In the traditional manner of the imperial court, his teeth were blackened. *The Standard*, a British newspaper, wrote of his "antique manly beauty," *The Westminster Gazette* of his "calm, dignified composure."

Born and raised in the isolation of the Kyoto court, the boy ruler, acknowledged as the 122nd emperor of Japan, was easily manipulated by forces wishing to use his status to shift power and lead Japan into the modern age. Emperors had always been shadow figures, stripped of any meaningful political leverage, but were revered as divinities due to the belief that they were directly descended from the sun goddess Amaterasu Omikami, the "great divinity illuminating heaven."

To promote his visibility, the new emperor, again dressed in sumptuous court robes, was carried across the moat into Edo Castle by palanquin the next year. His reign was named Meiji, or "Enlightened Rule." The bewitching rituals and heraldry of court, the unassailable eminence of tradition, the power of rank, and the conceit of those who held high position were not swept away, but recalibrated for a new age. The transformations of the period, in which many of the trappings of the ancient regime were discarded, were apparent in the appearance of the emperor himself. On the occasions he was not being shielded from public gaze, he now crossed the moat in a European carriage, made public addresses, visited factories, inspected his troops, and dressed in a Western military uniform replete with braiding and piping. It was a carefully crafted public-relations campaign designed to show that the emperor's rule was firmly dedicated to progress.

Likewise, government officials were now required to exchange their native clothes for Western ones, at least in public. Men, including samurai, were obliged to shave their heads and wear their hair in the Western manner. Something similar had occurred in Moscow in 1698, when Peter the Great, freshly returned from Amsterdam, had ordered his subjects to cut their beards and moustaches. The Czar had even gone so far as to post barbers at the gates of the capital, forbidding entry to the city unless visitors underwent compulsory shavings. Such draconian measures were not necessary in Japan, where people were still accustomed to obeying authority.

The samurai had evolved from warriors into a class of minor administrators and social parasites, their monthly stipends a drain on the national coffers. The abolishment of their ranks and stipends made their humiliation complete, and left them equipped with few practical skills for the new age. Penury descended particularly on the pro-shogunate samurai, who were forced to make a living working as servants in foreign households, pulling rickshaws, and selling off antiques and items of used clothing—vestiges of their own former status. The dilapidation of the old system could be seen in the condition of abandoned aristocratic estates, many now turned over for the cultivation of tea bushes and mulberry trees. The first government offices were housed in these spacious Edo mansions.

Time itself changed, with the introduction of the Gregorian calendar, replacing a lunar one in which the day was divided into twelve horary signs, whose lengths were subject to either winter or summer daylight. Edo was renamed Tokyo in July 1868. In the same year, Edo Castle was renamed Tokyo Castle and adapted for use as the emperor's residence after his move from Kyoto in 1869.

With the fall of the shogunate and the system of *sankin kotai* in 1862, samurai from rural fiefs returned to their provincial seats, and the population of the main districts dropped by roughly 300,000. It had rebounded to 885,000 by 1882 and rose to over a million the next year. The sharp demographic resurgence was due in part to the influx of descendants of former samurai clans coming to Tokyo looking for employment as public servants, schoolteachers, and patrolmen. Flophouses and split-row homes sprang up to cater to a stream of peasants from the countryside displaced by the social upheavals.

From being isolated from public events by a long line of military dictators, distracted from engaging in national affairs by an endless round of time-consuming ceremonies, the new emperor was suddenly a manifestly active figure, still a living deity but a man with decisive ideas about the direction of the nation. Shinto and emperor-worship were fused by decree. Buddhist ceremonies were eliminated from the palace, creating an opportunity to further promote the cult of emperor-worship. At a stroke, feudalism had been replaced with the reinvigoration of a system of divinity dating back two millennia. Emperor-worship as an integral part of Japanese nationalism, however, would compromise the avowed aim of Meiji progressiveness to create a more open and accountable form of government seeking more public participation. In practice, the emperor was accountable to powerful reformist politicians like Okubo Toshimichi and Ito Hirobumi, who set the agenda in his name.

The young emperor announced that knowledge would be sought throughout the world. This very pragmatic declaration was followed by a series of stirring slogans, such as *Bunmei kaika* ("Civilization and Enlightenment"), *Fukoku kyohei* ("A Rich Nation and a Strong Army"), and *Wakon yosai* ("Japanese Spirit and Western Culture"). The nation was faced with the choice of having to either modernize existing traditions or traditionalize an emerging modernity. Thus began a period of avid assimilation and ingestion that continues to this day.

Once set in motion, change proceeded rapidly. The government quickly confiscated large tracts of land on which daimyo properties stood, allocating them as administrative office buildings and military quarters. By 1869, telegraph lines were operating between Tokyo and Yokohama, and railway tracks were laid between Shinbashi and Yokohama in 1872; a telephone service was introduced in 1877. Female telephone-exchange operators were pioneers of Japan's first generation of working women.

A waterworks survey was conducted in 1876; a port construction was undertaken in 1880—all part of an effort to consolidate Tokyo's position as the country's capital. Comparing the late Edo-period prints of Hiroshige with those of his student Hiroshige III reveals a radical change in content. Artists like Hiroshige III, Kiyochika, and Yoshitora show us forceful aspects of modern life in their street scenes: pedestrians in Western dress, wheeled traffic, brick-and-stone hotels and banks, gas lamps, European-style shopping streets, steam trains, omnibuses, and factories belching black plumes of smoke as satanic as anything found in Lancashire or the rust belts of North America.

A fine example of the new congestion and excitement gripping the city is Utagawa Hiroshige III's brightly illustrated three-part panel entitled "Scenic View of Tokyo Enlightenment," conceived in 1874. The static elements include the Kyobashi bridge, the Ginza's new brick-and-stone shops, and the reassuring backdrop of Mount Fuji. The main activity of the panel is the exuberant street life. A number of fully dressed rickshaw-pullers move across this lively triptych (only a few years earlier, such men had gone about their business naked from the waist up). The river below the bridge is visible, but there is no activity on it. In one of the most notable transformations of the Meiji period, all the activity of the city has risen from its sunken watercourses to street level.

The Edo-period board game *sugoroku*, in which players threw dice and moved from frame to frame along an illustrated itinerary equivalent to a sightseeing tour of the city, underwent a telling change in Meiji times. Famous places were replaced with the theme of *shusse-sugoroku* ("climbing the social ladder"). Its illustrated route—progressing from images of peddlers and rickshaw drivers, advancing past the entrances of well-to-do merchants, and terminating in elite club houses and chambers of council—depicted the boundless hopes and ambitions of the new age.

In the first years of the Meiji era alone, some 50 to 60,000 young men, poor students known as *shosei*, arrived in Tokyo to enjoy its new culture and seek their fortunes. Many worked as live-in manservants in order to pay their way through school. The desire to rise in the world took on a delusional aspect, with parents expecting their sons to "become a doctor or cabinet minister one day." One contemporary song expressed a common fantasy: "To drink yourself to sleep on the lap of a beauty, and to wake up sober at the helm of the state."

Buildings would be needed to match these vaulting aspirations. As architecture was synonymous in people's minds with advanced Western culture, creating a Westernized cityscape became identified as the hallmark of a civilized nation. At the same time that Georges-Eugene Haussmann was redesigning the center of Paris, Tokyo—with no master planner this time—was setting about deconstructing itself. The great Meiji building bazaar would turn the city into something akin to an Expo site, an emporium of construction styles. Early practitioners of architecture recreated European models of modernization, bringing about an efflorescence of brick banks, schools, post offices, town halls, bridges, furnaces, and train stations that would utterly transform the urban landscape.

The changes to Tokyo were most noticeable in individual buildings that stood out as beacons of modernity, rather than in entirely reconceived zones. While the trappings of Westernization—in the form of missionary schools, horse-drawn carriages, even the odd velocipede—were visible in the foreign settlement at Tsukiji, an area of reclaimed land close to the bay, the area's best-known sight was the Tsukiji Hoterukan, known to Westerners as the Edo Hotel. Crowds of Japanese sightseers came to see this symbol of new civilization, which was completed in the autumn of 1868. More than a hundred woodblock prints commemorated its opening; a slew of color prints followed in 1869 and 1870. A triptych by the prominent artist Utagawa Kuniteru II depicts merchants making deliveries in the bustling forecourt, with a Japanese flag fluttering in the background beside Akashi Bridge. A contemporary photograph confirms the accuracy of Kuniteru's rendition.

The hotel was the work of a former carpenter named Shimizu Kisuke II, who had also worked as a building contractor in the foreign settlement at Yokohama. Japanese carpenters, imitating the pseudo-Western *giyofu* style, liked to transpose the decorative eclecticism popular in Europe while adding on local motifs like dragons, clouds, and phoenixes to buildings. Cupolas, towers, and turrets were common. The timber frame of the Tsukiji

Hoteru-kan—as well as its tiled roof, dark outer walls crisscrossed with plaster patterning, and bell tower reminiscent of traditional castles—was essentially Japanese in execution, though Western features were incorporated in the form of an expansive veranda vaguely reminiscent of British Raj architecture, sash windows, and European-style furnishings.

Many Meiji-era structures, conspicuous with ornamentation, have a toy model appearance. The reasons for their diminutive scale is not clear, but it may have been a result of limited land availability; economic caution at a time when the future was by no means certain; the cost of working with materials like brick, stone, and glass; or the sense that these were experiments in architecture with no assurances of longevity. The Japanese accepted these hybrids, while foreigners were more perplexed by the conflation of styles, perhaps feeling a little like a modern observer gazing up at a skyscraper fitted out with Etruscan pillars. As prime examples of the new architecture, buildings like this represented a strong urge to embrace the future combined with a reluctance to completely disengage from the past. Tokyo's experiments with Western-inspired architecture and other urban accretions, which would lead to an extraordinary jumble of styles and not a few visual dissonances, were apparent in the Ginza's mishmash of gas lamps, paved sidewalks, willow trees, and telegraph poles.

After a fire broke out inside the old castle compound at the headquarters of the Army Department in late February, 1872, flames spread rapidly eastward toward the bay and the Ginza district, fanned by high winds. Thousands of buildings and almost 100 hectares of land at the center of the city were razed.

The Great Ginza Fire created an opportunity to modernize the district, which had become increasingly important for its location between the major railhead at Shinbashi and the commercial district of Nihonbashi. What emerged from this ambitious project was the Ginza Brick Quarter, designed by the Irish architect and civil engineer Thomas James Walters. It took almost a decade to create what was intended to be a fireproof showcase for modern Tokyo. On completion, there were more than a thousand brick buildings running across the contiguous Ginza and Kyobashi areas. The country's first sidewalks were installed, and the street itself, now widened as a firebreak, was paved with brick.

It should have been a proud showcase for Meiji-era progress and development, had it not been for all the problems that quickly beset the area. Badly ventilated buildings, ill-suited to the semitropical humidity of Tokyo summers, turned into breeding grounds for mosquitoes, centipedes, and lizards. All the magnificent trees save the willows died, and several residents suffered from edema. In despair, many people forsook the area, leaving rooms that were presently taken over, in the words of Paul Waley, by "acrobats, jugglers, and other itinerant entertainers—including dancing dogs and wrestling bears." The area became a mockery of the Meiji period's much-vaunted age of civilization and enlightenment, and only got back on its feet after the government offered special subsidies to induce people to return.

Foreigners pining for the atmosphere of London, Paris, Berlin, or St. Petersburg could now repair to the Café Lion, where European wines, whisky, and vodka could be ordered, along with good Japanese sake and beer. The entire social spectrum—from street-walkers, laborers, and students to embassy and legation officers, professors, lawyers, politicians, musicians, authors, and critics—could be seen eating and drinking on any given night in the most crowded spot, the downstairs bar.

For those who could afford it and had the right connections, Ginza evenings could be spent at a European-style gentleman's club like the Kojunsha, where the fine carriages waiting at the entrance in the early Meiji era gave way to Packards later on. Most members were graduates of Keio College, but statesmen, journalists, lawyers, and businessmen were also found among their numbers. With its billiard room, wine cellar, library, neatly set-out newspapers and periodicals, and a barbershop on the third floor, it was much like any European club, but with Japanese touches: tables set out for games of *shogi* and *go*, a room for practicing Japanese dance, and paintings by leading artists of the day hanging on the walls. Such clubs were often limited to affiliated circles. Hence, the Kazoku-kaikan was reserved for peers of the realm; the Nihon Club mostly for government officials; the Gakushikai to Imperial University graduates; and the 1913 Mitsui Club, the only building left standing today, for Mitsui employees. Among the other work-related establishments were the Boeki-Kyokai, for members of the trade association; the Tetsudo Kyokai, for railway association workers; and the Jugo Ginko Club, catering to staff from the No. 15 Bank. The Tokyo Club was open to both peers and foreigners.

Countless restaurants and teahouses could be found in the Ginza. Along the alleys adjacent to the restaurants and teahouses were rows of geisha houses; by the end of the Meiji era there were no fewer than sixty-six geisha establishments in the Ginza area alone. The neighborhood had other businesses, too. Anyone walking through the district after 1 a.m. would have heard a strange, irregular whirring sound emitting from some of the larger buildings. The noise came from the rotary presses of newspaper offices. By the end of the Meiji era, there were eight newspaper companies operating in the Ginza. Many of the journalists who worked inside these buildings were former shogunal vassals. Regarded as unfit to serve the new Meiji government, many of these disgruntled men, working for papers such as the *Yubin Hochi Shinbun* (*Mail Reporter*), and the *Tokyo Nichi Nichi Shinbun* (*Tokyo Daily News*), had reinvented themselves as champions of a seminal democratic-rights movement. As such, they were keen to use the new print form to foment anti-government views. Just before dawn, the sound of bells ringing could be heard as men pulled carts transporting the papers to distributors. For workaholics or revelers who found themselves in these streets in the early hours around dawn, this would have been a good time to catch one of the first trams of the day; the fare before 7 a.m. was half-price.

The structural development of key areas like the Ginza was greatly aided by the employment of *oyatoi-gaikokujin*, or foreign experts. It became clear that what Japan wanted from these experts and consultants was for them to transfer their skills to their eager Japanese understudies, and then, at the end of their allotted contracts, depart. They were invaluable assets to a developing country, but once their skills were acquired, they became expendable.

Many of the early European buildings designed by foreign architects have vanished. Among the most outstanding were the Engineering College auditorium executed by Frenchman C. de Boinville; the Army Memorial Hall, which was the work of the Italian designer G. V. Cappelletti; and American R. P. Bridgens's Shinbashi station building. Tokyo's public and commercial buildings of the time, glimpsed in postcards and photographs, bear a strong resemblance to Victorian structures—which, given the number of English architects and engineers invited to work in Tokyo, is hardly surprising. Josiah Conder, the best-known foreign architect of the Meiji era, arrived in Japan in 1877 at the invitation of the Ministry of Technology. Conder taught at the influential College of Technology, and managed to complete a great many architectural projects while maintaining a teaching post. These included the School for the Blind in Tsukiji and the 1881 Imperial Museum at Ueno, a Gothic, red brick building that incorporated arresting Islamic elements.

These exotic flourishes resurfaced in Conder's best-known design, the Rokumeikan. When Prime Minister Ito hosted a masquerade ball, the venue he selected for the occasion was the Rokumeikan. It was really the only choice possible for such an extravaganza. Its symmetrical brick-and-masonry facades were a fine example of Meiji-era syncretism—a mix of new Tokyo, European provincial, and French Second Empire; its exterior combined a number of Italian Renaissance themes characteristic of a fifteenth-century palazzo, with cupolas after the Mogul style, a miniature mansard roof, and segmented arches. Not to be outdone by the external flourishes, the interior consisted of a billiard room, a promenade hall, a suite for official state guests, a reading room, and a ballroom. The dining area was presided over by a French chef whose banquet menus included red-snapper casserole, roast quail, beef fillets with horseradish, and Hungarian-style leg of lamb. American cocktails and German beer could be ordered at the bars.

A French naval office by the name of Lieutenant L. M. Viaud—better known by his pen name, Pierre Loti, under which he wrote lyrical novels with exotic settings—attended the second annual ball of honor for the emperor's birthday in November 1885. Loti was unimpressed, comparing Conder's design to a second-rate casino of the kind found in French hot-spring resorts. The government had gone to some lengths to hire a German, one L. V. Janson von der Osten, to give lessons on a weekly basis at the Rokumeikan. The results were evidently not good enough for the testy Loti. Watching the guests going through their polkas, mazurkas, and waltzes, he concluded: "They dance quite properly, my Japanese in Parisian gowns. But one senses that it is something *drilled into* them, that they perform like automatons, without any personal initiative."

The French illustrator Georges Bigot, whose anti-government sentiments and pitiless satires caused him a good deal of harassment from the police, gleefully lampooned the acquired mannerisms of the Rokumeikan ladies and the contrived façade of Westernization the building tried to promulgate. His caricatures of a Japanese couple aping Western fashion, "The Elite of the Japanese World," depict simian-like figures grappling with a quadrille on the dance floor—a painfully exaggerated visualization of the desperate aspirations the Rokumeikan represented. In one image, four ladies in Western clothes take a break between dance lessons at the hall, but seem to have relapsed into Edo ways, striking unrefined poses—one figure squatting in the traditional manner, others enjoying a smoke from slender old-fashioned pipes called *kiseru*.

Prime Minister Ito's fancy dress ball was designed to be the pinnacle of high-society Tokyo life. When his guests arrived, conservative anti-government elements were shocked to see Japanese dignitaries dressed up as characters ranging from Doctor Faust and Mary Queen of Scots to Mother Hubbard. Persian and Egyptian themes were well represented among the four hundred guests. Mingling with women dressed in Louis XIV court dresses were imaginative caricatures, including an Oscar Wilde figure accompanied by two votaries. Ito himself came as a Venetian nobleman, his wife as a Spanish lady in a yellow silk dress and mantilla; their daughter turned up as an Italian peasant girl. Such a spectacle, inconceivable only a few years earlier, bespoke great and formative change. It was an age when men like Ito, in imitation of their Victorian counterparts, grew luxuriant moustaches and hung gold watch chains from their waistcoat pockets. (The watches were significant, for time itself was changing: city residents had always depended on temple bells for temporal matters.)

Conder had found an imaginative and indulgent sponsor in the Iwasaki family. He completed the first brick buildings for the company in 1894, in a wild tract of undergrowth east of the palace known as the Mitsubishi wasteland. People wondered what could be done with the desolate expanse, which was known as the habitat of foxes and stealthy thieves. The Iwasakis, who knew exactly what could be done with it, went along with the bemusement, even joking that they might cultivate a bamboo forest there and introduce tigers.

The four-story red-brick structures, faced with white quoins, were built in a quarter that came to be known as London Block, which featured lined streets boasting a very modern civic mix of trees and electric poles. As examples of transplanted town planning, they were, arguably, less successful. Cultural geographer Paul Waley captured the dissonance when he described these Marunouchi-area blocks as having

> …a late-Victorian London air of Marylebone High Street or parts of Kensington, but without the architectural conviction and spontaneity that grows out of native soil. Photographs of the London Block in its early days reveal a pronounced sense of unease. The buildings need carriages and trolleys and the bustle of late-Victorian and Edwardian London. Instead, all they have to look out on is a few rickshaws and the occasional disoriented passer-by.

Diminutive by today's standards, these buildings were considered tall. In Japan, height had always been synonymous with power and mystique. Sacred mountains were worshipped, the tallest shrine-trees revered; towering castle keeps were intended to impress, pagodas to suggest the celestial reaches. One of Tokyo's most remarkable buildings was the twelve-story Ryounkaku (Cloud-Surpassing Pavilion), which was destined to become the symbol of the Asakusa entertainment district and was much reproduced in postcards. Constructed in 1890 under the supervision of the Scottish sanitary engineer William Kinnimond Burton, the 216-foot octagonal tower, replete with 176 windows, was the tallest building in Tokyo. Its floors were packed with imported goods, restaurants, and an observation deck equipped with telescopes; the ninth floor was reserved for art exhibitions. It boasted Japan's first elevator. More than just a building, the Ryounkaku was an early symbol of mass culture and entertainment. In a wonderfully embellished print by Kunisada Utagawa, the air space around the tower is swarming with kites, balloonists, and parachutists; a figure appears to be taking an exuberant leap from one of its floors into the air.

The new Imperial Palace, designed by Japanese architects headed by Kigo Kiyotaka, was completed in 1889. Reverting to a classic Japanese style of architecture, it had a series of linked wooden pavilions and covered passages overlooking courtyard gardens. The syncretism of the age gained purchase in the form of brick chimneys, parquet floors, flowered carpets, and Victorian furniture. If architecture can be metaphor, the palace served well for the times—the emperor appeared in the public wing dressed as a modern monarch in the uniform of a field marshal, while in the west wing he would change into the traditional Japanese attire that most of his own people still wore. Ancient rites linking the Son of Heaven and the nation to his ancestors were performed in Shinto shrines at the rear of the palace; for these, the emperor would dress in court robes. Fitting a monarch synonymous with enlightenment, the palace had its own generator; the emperor was the first person in Japan to have his residence bathed in electric light.

A number of these Meiji-era constructions are still extant, among them Conder's Nikolai Cathedral in Ochanomizu. The playwright Hasegawa Shigure sometimes stayed with an aunt in the Kanda district, where she got a glimpse of the new world emerging on her doorstep:

> She took me to view the Nikolai Cathedral, which was then still under construction. It was during my stays at my aunt's home that I first had the chance to hear the sound of violin and piano and orchestra. In the district of the Low City where we lived, such sounds and such instruments were virtually unknown. So it was that I caught my first scent of the West.

The "scent of the West" would have been distinctly more potent if Hasegawa had stepped into the cathedral itself. Here, the iconostasis (altar screen) was ablaze with devotional paintings sent from Russia, and gold crosses stood arrayed in the light from the stained-glass windows. The faintly Byzantine exterior—more mosque than Russian Orthodox—betrayed Conder's hand, whose taste for the Moorish and Saracenic styles had, on occasion, to be moderated by his paymasters. Though the cathedral is encroached on today by shabby discount stores and nondescript office blocks, it is still possible to glimpse its dome and gain a hint of its once-dominant place on the Tokyo skyline.

A stronger scent of the West could be sensed at Tsukiji, where a foreign settlement was built. The settlement opened in 1869, but didn't find its feet until the following year. It was close to Shinbashi, site of the planned terminus for the railroad to Yokohama, and was accessible by boat to Yokohama. Foreigners billeted in its vaguely Western-style wooden homes would, by dint of its location in the still-remote lower Sumida area, be cut off from the centers of plebian and aristocratic Tokyo. This would be the very reason for its eventual desertion. After the Ginza fire of 1872, many foreigners left the settlement in favor of Yokohama, leaving Tsukiji to teachers, missionaries, and diplomats working at foreign legations. The settlement survived until the abrogation of extraterritoriality in July 1899, after which foreigners could decide for themselves where they wished to live.

Tsukiji's foreign missionaries had an influence that went beyond the settlement, traceable to the founding of Aoyama Gakuin University, Rikkyo University, Meiji Gakuin University, and Joshi University, among others. Fukuzawa Yukichi, a retainer of the Matsudaira clan, had set up a school of Western learning—the forerunner of Keio University—as early as 1858 in Tsukiji. Fukuzawa was a reformist liberal whose books, such as his 1872 *Gakumon no Susume* (An Encouragement of Learning), were avidly read by a literate public hungry for new ideas. The Meiji government, eager to modernize and strengthen infrastructures, but less given to social reform, were leery of Fukuzawa's declaration, "Heaven created no man above another, nor below."

An independent intellectual of the highest order, Fukuzawa was, nonetheless, a man of his time and upbringing. Held up to closer scrutiny, his proclamation of universal parity rings a little hollow. In his widely read 1885 essay, "Forget Asia," his barely disguised contempt for China and Korea are clear. The Chinese, he wrote, "are mean-spirited and without shame." Koreans he observed to be capable of excessive cruelty. Characterizing both of these neighboring nations as undeveloped, and therefore unworthy of a true alliance with Japan, he advised his countrymen to "cast its lot with the civilized nations of the West." Japan, following Fukuzawa's council, would emulate European colonial models that would, by the middle of the next century, be on the verge of obsolescence. Like the British, French, and Dutch, Japan would become an imperial power exercising regional hegemony at the expense of its subject peoples. Arguably more damaging in the long run for Japan—and something that it is still dealing with today in its troubled relations with neighboring countries—was the fact that while occupying parts of the Asian continent, it would, as Fukuzawa advocated, also disengage itself from the values of Asia.

More immediately beneficial than theories of Western alignment and imperial expansion were the stunning commercial advances of the day. Given the natural entrepreneurial skills of its residents, Edo was a global marketplace in waiting. The Mitsui family's wealth had come from banking services for the shogun and their dry goods store Echigoya. By the early twentieth century, Echigoya had turned into Mitsukoshi, Japan's first Western-style department store. Like its American counterpart, Wanamaker's, its attraction was not in simply selling commodities, but in promoting culture through seasonal exhibitions and displays. Other stores quickly followed Mitsukoshi's example. Shirokiya, located close to Mitsukoshi and with a similar history as an Edo institution, was the second department store to open. As establishments like Takashimaya and Mitsukoshi opened stores in the Ginza and Kyobashi districts, these areas developed into major retailing centers. Maruzen, a leading bookstore, opened in the Nihonbashi district in 1869, offering titles in both Japanese and foreign languages.

Commerce required new forms of transportation, and these would inevitably be supplied by the West. A foreign loan was raised from the United Kingdom to finance the construction of a railway line between Yokohama and Shinagawa in Tokyo in 1872. Under the supervision of chief engineer Edmund Morel, British technicians and 114 mostly British overseers, foremen, engine drivers, boilermakers, blacksmiths, and Japanese manual workers laid a 24-kilometer line, which was extended during the summer of the same year to Shinbashi.

Somewhere between 60,000 and 100,000 people turned up for the opening ceremony, which had a palpable European flavor. The emperor arrived in an open barouche built by the London company Lawrie and Marvell; the melody for the new national anthem, composed by the English bandmaster John W. Fenton, was sung; and a bevy of journalists, including several from the foreign press, then joined His Majesty for the trip to Yokohama. It was probably the last time he appeared on such an occasion dressed in ancient court robes. The empress, holding a parasol, chose to appear in a formal Western dress. The British railway officials who greeted the emperor in Yokohama were attired in top hats and frock coats, as if attending a formal garden party hosted by Queen Victoria. It was one of Japan's first crowd-pleasing costume dramas, which the period learned to stage with great flair.

When the train service opened in 1872, the lowest of the three categories of train tickets still cost nine times the pay of an average laborer. Trains were a symbol of progress, and strict instructions on train conduct were issued by the government. Footwear was not to be removed before entering the carriages, and anyone caught urinating out of the windows would be subject to a fine. Peasants in the rural areas between the two cities, watching the trains roaring between their fields, referred to the engines as *karyu*, "fire dragons," and would, on occasion, kneel in deference as they passed.

New woodblock prints soon appeared depicting snorting locomotives passing by paddy fields with Mount. Fuji in the background. Trains were part of the new commercial city, the mechanization that brought the roar of progress with it. The poet Shiki Masaoka, a resident of the quiet downtown Tokyo district of Negishi, captured the disruption inflicted on the city's remaining traces of stillness in a tanka composed in 1900:

> Glimpsed in luminous moonlight
> the woods of Ueno—
> then my home shaken and rattled
> by passing locomotives

The cork that had sealed the realm of Japanese literature and ideas in an airtight insularity burst off. Into this world—hitherto defined by Buddhism, Confucianism, Shinto, and a good deal of superstition—came Nietzche's unsparing critique, Ibsen's dramas, Tolstoy's ego, and Zola's social dissection. Other writers like Kant and Hegel were avidly read by graduates, intellectuals, and free thinkers. In the next era, serious readers would be consulting the works of Kierkegaard, Von Hartmann, Heidegger, and a political theorist by the name of Karl Marx.

Intellectual discourse could be relieved by any number of other forms of stimulation. In the beginning it seemed as if the illustrious actors who had performed Noh would not survive the removal of their samurai rank, and there were eyewitness accounts of once-venerated artists working as basket vendors on the roadsides. Once it was realized that Noh might serve as a showcase for the Japanese arts, much as opera and ballet did in the West, however, efforts were set in motion to resuscitate the form. Members of the Meiji nobility built a Noh theater in Shiba Park in 1881, and four of the Noh schools, led by the Kita and Kanze families, constructed public theaters in Tokyo.

Determined to sanitize Kabuki, the actor Ichikawa Danjuro IX, wearing a swallowtail coat, delivered a speech before the audience of the new Shintomi-za, declaring:

> Theater in recent years has consumed filth and has reeked of the coarse and the mean. I, Danjuro, am deeply grieved. In consultation with my colleagues, I have resolved to remove the decay.

In an effort to gain greater social respectability for Kabuki, the Three Theaters moved to more prestigious addresses in places like east Ginza, abandoning their Low City audiences. Five new Kabuki theaters were built in Tokyo in 1873, most located in the high city. A Society for Theater Reform presented ideas for the "improvement" of Kabuki. Endorsing the new, reformed Kabuki, the Meiji emperor attended a performance in 1887—an act that would have been unthinkable a mere twenty years earlier.

The emperor's hand touched that of a Westerner for the first time on July 4, 1879, when he was formally introduced to Ulysses S. Grant, the former U.S. president. Some days thereafter, on July 16, the Grants attended a Kabuki gala in their honor at the prestigious Shintomi-za Theater. Among those selected to sit with the Grants in the dress circle was a young American woman named Clara Whitney, who recorded the sight of a dance line of Shinbashi geisha:

> Each girl was dressed in a robe made of the dear old Star and Stripes, while upon their heads shone a circlet of silver stars...their girdles were dark blue, sandals, red and white, and presently they took out fans having on one side the American and upon the other the national flag.

It was an extraordinary mix of entertainment and goodwill diplo-

CHAPTER 3

macy. Grant had donated a new curtain to the theater. The great
Kabuki actor Danjuro stepped onto the stage in a frock coat to
thank the honored guest for his generosity. The appearance of a
Kabuki actor dressed in this manner was telling.

One of the most extraordinary figures in the Tokyo entertainment world of this time was an Australian by the name of Henry
James Black, whose father was a well-known publisher. Black,
with his heart set on being an entertainer, became a pupil of the
famous *kodanshi* (narrative storyteller) Shorin Hakuen. Black's
early appearances at *yose* (music halls) created a sensation among
audiences intrigued by the sight of a foreigner—a fluent Japanese
speaker no less—relating stirring tales of historical figures like
Joan of Arc and Charles I. He went on to study *rakugo*, a performing art that evolved from *kodan* (storytelling), with the influential
Sanyutei family. Its leading member, Sanyutei Encho, enjoyed the
company of a wide range of writers. This helped Black produce
more considered stories, like the supernatural *Tale of the Peony
Lantern*. He also enjoyed integrating and adapting works from
Western culture, like de Maupassant's story *A Parricide*, into
his *rakugo* repertoire. Taking the stage name Kairakutei, Henry
even went on to perform as an *onnagata* (female impersonator)
on the Kabuki stage. His first role was Chobei in the play *Ban-
zuin Chobei*.

Women reemerged on the male-dominated stage after the
government rescinded a ban on the public performance of females in 1877. Women quickly took to the stage as musician-
singers known as *gidayu*. Providing a musical and narrative
accompaniment at puppet theaters, their sumptuous kimonos
were soon replaced by men's trousers and tops. Young men from
Tokyo universities formed fan clubs centering on their favorite
performers. In 1900, the authorities, just as fearful as their Edo
forbears had been of the supposedly corrupting influence of
women in theaters, introduced an ordinance prohibiting male
students from attending *gidayu* shows.

Along with theatrical forms and fashions came a menagerie of exotic animals introduced by foreigners. A tidy profit was made by the Dutch in the Straits of Malacca when they bought two tigers for $100 and resold them for $3,000 to the Japanese for an exhibition. There was great excitement when a Portuguese entrepreneur introduced a three-year-old Indian elephant early in 1863. The female pachyderm, exhaustively reproduced in prints over the winter and early spring, was exhibited in the old Ryogoku entertainment district. Kanagaki Robun, a satirical journalist, wrote the commentary for a diptych by Utagawa Yoshitoyo, in which he visualized the arrival of exotic creatures as a form of tribute, claiming, "The glory of our holy land has spread even abroad and rare things and strange birds and beasts of foreign countries are offered to us." Kanagaki saw the elephant as a bearer of supernatural powers, claiming:

> It understands what people say and it can guess their feelings; it puts out fires and drives out harmful pestilences. It gets rid of poisonous things. For those who see it, the seven misfortunes will decrease and the seven fortunes will grow.

The Cirque Soullier, run by a sixty-two-year-old Frenchman of the same name, brought its equestrian act to Yokohama in 1871. In December the troupe performed to great acclaim at Shokonsha, now the grounds of Yasukuni Shrine in Kudanshita. More regular equestrian events took place at the racetrack that circled Shinobazu Pond in Ueno. The emperor attended the opening of the track in November 1884. In prints celebrating the event, we see officials pressed tight into the bleachers, festive boats floating on the pond, and fireworks blasted from bamboo cannons. The racecourse only lasted for ten years, and its construction greatly damaged the natural beauty of the area.

By the early 1870s, there were many portrait photographers

with their own studios working in Tokyo and Yokohama. A lucrative trade in images of popular geisha and actors could be seen in street booths. Japan wasted no time in developing a seminal cinema industry. The Cinématographe Lumièr was imported as early as 1897; shortly afterwards, Thomas Edison's Vitascope could be seen in the capital. The photographer Asano Shiro imported the first motion-picture camera the same year, and was soon documenting Tokyo street scenes. The Mitsukoshi department store established its own film department, sending its cameramen out to record Ginza street life and geisha. Ticket prices were high, but there were no problems in selling seats at the Kabuki-za theater for screenings of geisha dances captured by the newly formed Association of Japanese Motion Pictures. The Japan Cinematograph Company, later known as Nikkatsu, opened a large new studio in Mukojima, on the east side of the Sumida River. By 1914, the company was producing an impressive fourteen films a month. Early newsreels appeared at this time.

The hot stream of humanity that flowed into Asakusa invariably passed through the Senso-ji temple grounds, where there was sufficient space for all manner of entertainment, very little of it pertaining directly to the spiritual. An 1871 woodblock print by Utagawa Hiroshige depicts some of the acts performed by the Grand French Equestrian Troupe in the temple compound. Another, dated 1887 and executed by Utagawa Yoshimori, shows pilgrims climbing the circular path of a replica Mount Fuji. Located near the temple in the Hanayashiki district, the structure served—besides its obvious novelty value—as a substitute pilgrimage for the elderly, disabled, or penurious, who were not able to make the journey to the actual peak; and for women, who, because of their ritual impurity, were not allowed to. From the summit, the real Mount Fuji could be seen on the horizon.

The pleasure quarters continued to provide their own forms of entertainment and diversion in much the same manner as they had in their Edo heyday, though it was now common to see

Westerners wandering the willow-lined streets of the quarter. A. B. Mitford visited the Yoshiwara in the 1870s, finding it largely intact. Nightfall, he maintained, was the best time to attend; one would see women seated "side by side, in a kind of long narrow cage, the wooden bars of which open to the public thoroughfare. Here they sit for hours, gorgeous in dresses of silk and gold and silver embroidery, speechless and motionless as wax figures."

Change was coming to the quarter, however, not just in the appeals for reform from women's rights activists like Hiratsuka Raicho, but from writers like Higuchi Ichiyo, who described the lives of young children living near the perimeter of the Yoshiwara and its black ditch, and from a public aware of how vulnerable such quarters were to criticism from less tolerant visitors than Mitford. A law was passed in 1900 allowing the women of the licensed quarters to leave of their own volition. Eleven hundred women of the Yoshiwara did just that, depleting its numbers almost overnight and causing a number of hitherto prosperous houses to close down.

The quality of the clientele at the Yoshiwara appears to have declined during this period as well, with the appearance of a new breed of ruffian and drunkard, ignorant of the etiquette of the quarter. Men working at the lower-level houses of the district would have to avoid being dragged into brawls that sometimes turned violent. Their wives would strike flints behind them as they departed for work, the spark both purification and ritual protection against evil. The writer Nagai Kafu, returning to the quarter after spending some years abroad, was dispirited by the lack of attention to the poetic seasonal details the Yoshiwara was renowned for, as well as by the shocking sight of Western-style beer halls. "I felt like a faded habitué," he wrote, "witnessing a world that had been inverted."

For those who could afford them, the two most fashionable geisha quarters were located in the Shinbashi (New Bridge) and Yanagibashi (Willow-Tree Bridge) districts. Men of more slender means could visit Fukagawa, which boasted no less than seven unlicensed pleasure quarters. Located beyond the jurisdiction of the city, its more costly prostitutes erroneously referred to themselves as geisha. A feature of the Fukagawa prostitutes was their refusal to wear *tabi*, the white socks worn with kimonos, even on bitter winter days. Doing so would have concealed their toenails, which they painted red—a color associated with the erotic.

Entertainment and mass culture were moderated by determined national ambitions, which were evident in the rousing mottos, rallying calls, and slogans of the day. One that sounded more like a directive than a hopeful urging was *Oitsuke oikose!* ("Catch up and surpass!") This catchphrase embodied the aspirations of the times very well. The fact that electric lights were installed in large factories well before they appeared in private homes highlighted the urgency given to prioritizing industry. In an effort to turn Tokyo into a showcase capital that would— among other things—impress the growing number of foreigners coming to Japan, model factories, heavily dependent on foreign equipment and advisors, were set up. Fukagawa had a cement factory, a chemical fertilizer plant, a Western-style shipyard, textile factories, even a sugar refinery. Oji had its paper-processing operations; Shinagawa a glass plant; Honjo a number of leatherworks, matchstick manufacturers, and even a factory where railway carriages were built.

This growth supported an expanding population. From an estimated 500,000 residents in the 1860s, Tokyo's population had doubled by the 1890s. By 1907 it had reached two million, rising to three million by 1920. During these decades of industrial and commercial growth, huge numbers of migrants from rural areas poured into the city looking for work. Many were successful in finding jobs, but the pay and conditions were often dismal. New neighborhoods appeared on the city's peripheries, while existing areas became unbearably crowded.

The paper mill and factory that had been set up in the suburb of Oji in 1875 created a large slum zone that housed many of its workers and their families. In neighborhoods along the Sumida River, where new industries sprang up like poisoned mushrooms, unsanitary slums were common. Adding to the residential mix in these zones were criminals, street performers, beggars, the unemployed, destitute migrants, assorted drifters, and members of the so-called naked occupations like rickshaw pullers and laborers. The three largest ghettos were Shitaya Mannecho in the north, Shiba Shinamicho to the south, and the western Yotsuya Samegabashi district. Known as *hinminkutsu*, meaning "poor people's caves," these were soon being referred to as *suramu*, the Japanese rendition of the English word "slum."

While the drawing rooms of the wealthy were lit by bright electric lights, most Tokyo residents lived in semi darkness. As the population expanded, the majority of residents living in deplorable conditions, the city began to reek. Part of the problem was the obstacles encountered with waste disposal. By the late Meiji era, the city had grown so large that the farms on its edges were too far away for the night-soil carts to transport human waste from the metropolitan areas. When it rained, the human sewage used to fertilize rice paddies ran into rivers and canals, contaminating the water system, which in the Edo period had been the pride of the city. The poor water quality and attendant health risks were somewhat improved by the appointment at a Tokyo university in 1887 of Scotsman William Burton as professor of sanitary engineering. Burton's first concern was to improve the purification process with the use of sand filters. He also initiated the construction of reservoirs for fresh water storage.

Varying forms of urban existence and corresponding poverty became the object of intense study by writers, philanthropists, and what we would now call social workers. Like his European counterparts Mayhew, Booth, and Dickens, the writer Yokoyama Gennosuke attempted to bring the plight of Tokyo's three great slums to public attention in his book *Japan's Lower Classes*. Other titles like *In Darkest Tokyo*, by Matsubara Iwagoro, appeared as well.

If your pockets were truly threadbare, you could at least spend the night at a *kichinyado*, the lowest form of lodging house. Asakusa ward had plenty of accommodations like this; so did the sub-districts of Sarumachi, Nagazumicho, Hanacho, and Hiromachi. The highest concentration of such inns, though, could be found in the Tomikawacho district of Fukagawa ward, which listed 186 such houses in the last year of the Meiji era. Nearby Honjo ward had a large number as well. Laborers and night-stall keepers were the main clientele, sometimes staying for months on end, though visitors to the area often bought the services of streetwalkers there. For the truly destitute, there were a small number of free lodging houses called *muryo shukuhakujo*. These charitable establishments also helped the unemployed find work.

The lower reaches of the Sumida River, with its districts of thatchers, stonemasons, barrel-makers, plasterers, carpenters, and tailors, began incorporating new industries in the early years of the Meiji era, including factories where bricks, rickshaws, Western-style clothing, shoes, and roofing tiles were made. Larger production space was required for these enterprises, which could no longer be managed in cramped home shops. With increasing production, more industries were built along the upstream embankments of the Sumida River, especially in an area called Senju. The massive Senju Spinning Mill had already been built in 1879. By the turn of the century, the mill would employ almost 25,000 people. This was followed by the Tokyo Cardboard Company in 1886 and Tokyo Gas Company in 1893. Another huge industrial area was being actively developed in the 1890s at Keihin along Tokyo Bay.

Japan's version of the Industrial Revolution left women cruelly exploited as female factory workers living in crowded, unsanitary, evil-smelling dormitories. They were frequently underpaid, sexually abused, and beaten. The work was always hazardous; injury compensation, if paid at all, was trifling. Inside, the factories were hot, damp, and odiferous. It was not surprising that there was a high incidence of tuberculosis in these factories. Many young women, at the end of their tether, committed suicide. The factories were built in the naïve expectation that workers would retain their serf mentality—that farmers leaving their ancestral land holdings would remain at heart loyal peasants. The dawning of a proletariat enlightenment; the emergence of organizing plant managers, unions, and worker activism; and broader demands for civil rights, social reforms, and freedom of speech, assembly, and the press would put paid to that assumption. Even the most unschooled factory hand could hardly fail to realize that it was the abject poverty of the masses that provided new luxuries and novelties for the elite.

With nineteenth-century modernization came an immense change in the urban landscape, a transformation from soft to hard lines. The most literal and visible manifestation was the cobwebs of wires and utility poles that made a "horrid impression" on Lafcadio Hearn, a writer of Greek-Irish descent much given to self-pity, when he saw the city in 1897. By the 1880s, large parts of the Tokyo skyline were already festooned with telegraph wires and electric cables. Kite flying, a traditional pastime in Edo, was now deemed a risk and made illegal. It remains an offense in Tokyo to this day.

Ueno Park became the setting for a number of industrial fairs modeled on similar expositions held in Paris, Philadelphia, and London's Crystal Palace. Crowds of visitors flocked to the park, which became a kind of open campus for the acquisition of knowledge. For all the developments in industry, the talk of prog-ress and civilization and of addressing the conditions of the poor, improving the standing of women was not on the agenda of the new government. Prevailing conditions drove some women into embracing radical political ideologies, including anarchism, syn-dicalism, and Bolshevism. Fueling the early Meiji-era discussion on gender were translations of influential books such as Herbert

Spencer's 1877 *Social Statics* and, two years later, John Stuart Mill's *On the Subjection of Women*. The climate for advancement for both men and women was hobbled by draconian edicts such as the tightening of press and libel laws in 1877, and restrictions on public lectures, meetings, and debates—which the police attended—and the suppression of political journalism.

A feminist movement sprang up from literary interests under the stewardship of an extraordinary woman named Raicho Hiratsuka. The first issue of Raicho's magazine *Seito* (*Bluestocking*) on September 1, 1911, released a backlash that even Raicho could hardly have anticipated. Her rebellion against the irrationality that confined women was expressed in powerful imagery when she wrote:

> In the beginning, woman was the sun,
> An authentic person.
> Now, she is the moon,
> Existing through others.

Women interested in current affairs could read *Fujin Koron* (Women's Public Discourses) along with the more literary and radically inclined *Seito*. With its criticism of the traditional role of women, the family system, and marriage and its advocacy of free love, *Seito* could not fail to be controversial. In an article in an early issue, Raicho asked, "Why is it immoral to lose one's virginity? Why do people indiscriminately criticize unmarried women who lose their virginity?"

With the mastery of Western technology and skills, deference toward the West diminished by degrees as Japan became more confident in building a strong military and in defying the West by creating its own empire in the East. The political system fell short of being an outright dictatorship, but the new order that had overturned the feudalism of the *ancien regime* was an autocracy that brooked little dissent. Mori Arinori, the minister of education,

Top: Ancient burial mound, Todoroki.
Above: Entrance to Gokoku-ji temple.

Top: Edo period sake shop/storehouse.
Above: Meiji-era police box.
Opposite Top: Meiji-era missionary home in Zoshigaya.
Opposite Bottom: Iwasaki Mansion, Yushima.

Historical parade, Asakusa.

Matsuo Basho statue, Kiyosumi.

Merchant street, Edo period.

Kiyosumi temple, Ueno Park.

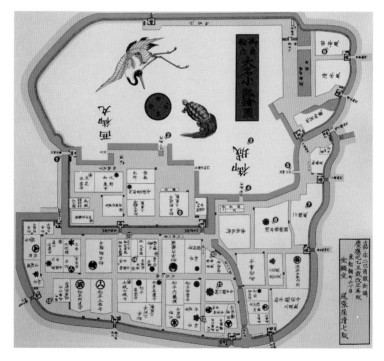

Top: Sumida River firework festival, Meiji era.
Above: Meiji-era print celebrating forms of transportation.
Opposite Top: Sumo wrestling in the Edo period.
Opposite: Edo-period map of Edo Castle.

Asakusa's twelve-story "skyscraper."

The Emperor Meiji.

活生の上の水

Top: Mourning the Emperor Meiji, Imperial Palace, 1912.
Above: Families living on boats, canal into the Sumida River.

Top: Mukojima, Taisho era.
Above: Imperial Hotel, Hibiya.

む望を越三りよ面側橋本日 (大東京)
Mitsukoshi Dept-store viewed from Nihonbashi (Great Tokyo)

Top: Nihonbashi bridge, Mitsukoshi dept. store, Taisho era.
Above: Eitaibashi bridge and industrial area, Taisho era.

Top: Ueno district, Taisho era.
Above: 1923 earthquake.

Top: Tokyo Station.
Above: Ginza, Taisho era.

Top: Asakusa pond.
Above: Taisho Exhibition site, 1913.

Top: Shirokiya store, Nihonbashi.
Above: Asakusa Kurumae-dori, early Taisho era.

Top: New Ginza Line subway.
Above: 1920s Tokyo, Denenchofu house.

Top: Zero fighter plane, Yasukan, Kudanshita.
Above: Emperor Hirohito, wartime period.

Top: Hibiya Crossing, 1948.
Above: Black market, Ginza, 1948.

Heron dance, Asakusa.

Top: The Edo era Denbo-in Garden, Asakusa.
Above: Tange's St.Mary's Cathedral, Mejirodai.

Top: National Art Center, Nogezaka.
Above: Aoyama Technical College.

Down and out in Sanya.

Top: Festival, Tsukiji.
Above: Water purifying rite, Kanda Myojin shrine.

Top: Dinosaur model, Shinjuku.
Above: New Year, Kanda Myojin.

Top: Ikebukuro.
Above: Islamic mosque, Yoyogi.
Opposite: Todoroki Gorge.

Top: Shopping center, Omotesando.
Above: Carbon Fiber Garden, Odaiba.

Hip hop street mural. Shibuya.

The "triple hollyhock" crest of the Tokugawa clan.

was assassinated in 1889 because of a supposed insult to the imperial shrine at Ise. The following year the moderate foreign minister Okuma, singled out for the slow handling of negotiations regarding treaty revision, was seriously injured when a bomb targeted him.

Empire-building had its detractors. Kotoku Shusui's 1901 book *Imperialism, the Monster of the Twentieth Century*, exposed the evils of colonialism. Kotoku was hanged, along with eleven others, after trumped-up charges accused him of attempting to assassinate the emperor. The military campaigns in occupied Korea and China, however, were popular with the public.

The 1904–05 Russo-Japanese War, like the Sino-Japanese War of 1894–95, enjoyed strong public support. With its conclusion and Japan's decisive victory, however, anger erupted in Hibiya Park, which became the site of violent protests expressing discontent with the unfavorable terms of the Treaty of Portsmouth, signed in September 1905, and the drop in the standard of living caused by the cost of the war. When it became known that Japan would not receive the indemnity it expected after waging a costly war that had brought the country to near bankruptcy, a swelling crowd of some 30,000 people ran rampant on the city. In the ensuing riots, police boxes were overturned, churches and streetcars set on fire, and shops looted in downtown Tokyo. The building housing the *Kokumin Shimbun*, a pro-treaty newspaper in the Izumo-cho district of Ginza, was set on fire. The eruption of violence led to seventeen recorded deaths and more than a thousand wounded, forcing the government to declare martial law. The emperor, shocked to hear shots fired by police who were trying to clear the park, cried, "The military police have fired on the people!" The rampages were quelled after the government placed the city under martial law.

A plot to assassinate the emperor was fomented by twenty-six conspirators who planned to bomb the imperial procession as it made its way to a military review in Aoyama. The subsequent trial was held *in camera* and with great dispatch. Death was in the air. A little over a year after the assassination attempt, the emperor, suffering from chronic nephritis and a worsening of his diabetes, collapsed. Crowds gathered in the open spaces around the palace to offer prayers for his recovery, many prostrating themselves on the ground. At forty-three minutes past midnight on July 30, 1912, the emperor died from heart failure.

Though two million people lined the route of the cortege, a respectful silence was observed on the night of his funeral, which took place on September 13. The auditory turmoil that was a feature of the Meiji period—the clanging tram-cars, humming telegraph wires, jackhammers, and factory horns—were muted for this period of mourning. Those observing it were as silent as ghosts as the city returned to the pre-mechanized world of Edo. Night fell, and procession torches, fueled with pine resin, were lit. The footsteps of the procession and the oxen pulling the catafalque were deadened by a two-foot-deep layer of sand that had been placed over all the roads along the route. The only audible sounds were footsteps in the sand, the labored breathing of oxen, and the creaking of the cart axles.

On the night of September 13, at the moment the guns of the Imperial Army signaled the departure of Emperor Meiji's cortege, General Nogi Maresuke, a flawed hero of the Russo-Japanese War, committed *junshi*, an ancient, little-practiced form of ritual suicide in which a retainer follows his lord in death. Before the general conducted his own disembowelment, he assisted his wife in severing her carotid artery. The public response was mixed, some criticizing the act as retrogressive, nationalists praising it as the ultimate expression of imperial fealty. The English-language press was no less divided over the incident. On the seventh anniversary of the general's death, the *Nippon Times* extolled the spirit of the act, while the *Japan Chronicle* reflected on "how much of this honor General Nogi would have received had he left behind him merely his reputation for high character, inflexible rectitude and military genius." Yajima Kajiko, a campaigner against brothels and a champion of a movement to cleanse public morals, was in awe of the general's wife, describing her suicide as an act of patriotism, a "beautiful deed, the true flowering of loyalty to a lord and love of country."

Skeptics who insisted there was little or no nobility in the act would have found support in a detail from the coroner's report that newspapers had assiduously omitted: Nogi had "inserted two cork-sized plugs into his rectum to prevent postmortem leakage." Whatever stand you took, no one denied that the death was a reproach to the betrayal of older values, which were about to enter into further decline with the new Taisho era.

The public's grief at the emperor's passing, its profound sense of loss, sprang from a personal identification between the emperor and his subjects, many of whom had been born during his long and transformative reign. The era had established Japan as the most advanced nation in Asia, but also acted as a breeding chamber for forms of state Shinto-linked imperialism, nationalism, and militarism that would eventually propel the country toward near-oblivion in World War II.

Not everyone had endorsed the great, wrenching changes. A young Tanizaki Junichiro, one of Japan's foremost literary figures, lamented the passing of the city's older physical fabric, writing, "Laid to waste by provincial samurai, this city of mine. No trace remains now of Edo as it was." The writer Nagai Kafu shared these sentiments. Casting an eye over the city that had risen from the impulses of the Meiji era, he wrote, "…when any city imitates the West to the same degree that Tokyo did, the resulting response from the observer is one of astonishment, along with a certain sense of pathos."

Judged in terms of good taste, the great Meiji bazaar was the best and worst of all times.

A lamp at the Meiji Shrine. Like so much of Tokyo's heritage, the original shrine was destroyed during World War II. Its rebuilding is an example of how, with the requisite will, tradition can stand side-by-side with progress. (Dreamstime © Ponsulak)

CHAPTER 4

The Flammable City

*Imperial decline – The great earthquake – Mass culture –
Radical politics – Social unrest*

"Bring down the snow, bring down the snow! Shallow or deep,"
female anarchist Kanno Sugako wrote in 1911: "Let it pile up so
high that this sinful city of Tokyo is smothered, like a city buried
in ash. Raze the entire landscape." The desire for self-destruction,
to be entombed beneath snow, ash, or worse, would come soon
enough, but for the present, other changes and upheavals in urban life and cityscape were afoot.

In writer Nagai Kafu's view, the markers signaling the end of
Edo and the fragility of whatever the city had managed to sal-
vage from the subsequent changes were two late-Meiji disasters:
the great Sumida River flood of 1910, which destroyed so much
of the Low City; and the fire the following year that razed the
Yoshiwara pleasure quarter. The nightless city recuperated as it
always had, but the cultural axis was moving in other directions.

Traces of an older city, however, still lingered in the upper
stretches of the Sumida River. In a 1916 woodblock print by the
artist Oda Kazuma, entitled *Scenes of Tokyo: The Sumida River
as Seen from Matsuchiyama*, both banks of the waterway, viewed
from an elevated graveyard, are green and verdant. Vessels plying
the route include one or two boats with canvas sails.

Still, progress and expansion were the rallying cries of the day. Trade and industrial exhibitions held in Tokyo were well supported by the public. Crowds also thronged the Colonial Exposition in Ueno, which began in October 1912, within the first months of the Taisho era. Among the appropriated treasures from the collection of Prince Yi of Chosen (Korea) were eighteen indigenous peoples, including aboriginals from the Japanese colony of Formosa (Taiwan) and an Ainu woman with blue facial tattoos from Japan's northern island of Hokkaido. The new emperor put in an appearance at another event, the Taisho Exposition, on June 18, 1914. Held to promote industry, it attracted an astounding seven million visitors. The emperor was seen leaving the event after buying a bag of jellybeans.

Because Meiji Empress Shoken had been barren, the emperor's son had been born to an imperial concubine. The new Taisho emperor apparently was something of a linguist, able to converse well in French, German, and English. Although he would later cut a rather eccentric figure—adopting, among other affectations, the waxed-handlebar mustache of Kaiser Wilhelm of Germany—Taisho was favorably regarded by the public at the beginning of his reign.

The emperor's progressive mental debility—the result in part of a bout of cerebral meningitis as an infant—and his physical frailty did not diminish his powerful sexual urges, which propelled him, even after becoming a divine sovereign, to regularly order attendants to procure women for him for the night. The effects of overindulgence and womanizing were exacerbated by persistent chain-smoking.

The low esteem in which he was held in both in court circles and within the corridors of the Diet, where he was mercilessly derided, would have great consequences. In a report to London on his initial impressions of Emperor Taisho after a meeting held in September 1912, Sir Claude MacDonald, the British ambassador, noted that, intellectually, the emperor was "generally supposed to be somewhat wanting and that is certainly the opinion the casual observer would arrive at after several moments' conversation." His public appearances became a subject of increasing embarrassment to the government. In 1921, the bedridden emperor was forced to transfer his duties to his son, Crown Prince Hirohito, who acted as regent until the emperor's death on Christmas Day in 1926.

After the death of Emperor Meiji, a monarch who had overseen a period of unparalleled change and created a legacy of power and wealth, the new reign began with a sense of unease and lassitude. Stepping into the vacuum was the evolution of greater social and personal freedoms, and the venting of grievances. A higher profile in national affairs was assumed by the press, who reported these developments, thereby creating a national forum for public opinion on all matters, including palace affairs. The decline of Emperor Taisho coincided with the Russian Revolution in 1917 and the collapse of monarchies in postwar Europe. A surge in wartime strikes in Japan, aided by a more politicized labor-union movement and the broadening appeal of Marxism to workers and intellectuals, created a groundswell of social and political radicalism that threatened to challenge even the imperial house. An unannounced increase in the price of rice saw some two million people take to the streets in the rice riots of August 1918, which were exacerbated by the insufferable heat of the Tokyo summer. Shops, police stations, high-end brothels, and churches were burned down, the homes of the rich looted. The authorities hanged the suspected ringleaders and arrested more than 25,000 rioters.

By 1920 Tokyo had lost its position as the largest and most populous city in the world, now ranking fifth after New York, London, Paris, and Chicago. But the city was bulging, its expanding population putting untoward pressures on transportation, water supply, and drainage systems, with housing shortages and spiraling rents causing social unrest. The total population stood at

3,700,000. The introduction of heavy industry had stimulated an influx of unskilled workers and laborers. Private commuter railway lines, zoning, building regulations, and the designation of an expanded Greater Tokyo Area were part of the City Planning Law and Urban Building Standards Act passed in 1919. Two years later, Mayor Goto Shimpei drew up and announced the optimistically named Outline of Tokyo City Administration, a hugely expensive scheme also known as the 800 Million Yen Project. Though ridiculed, the plan nonetheless provided a blueprint of what was required and how much it would take to implement the changes the city desperately needed. As it turned out, however, it was the uncontrollable forces of nature that would decide the future of Tokyo.

A strong northwest wind blew through the old bookseller's district of Kanda on February 19, 1913. By evening the winds had increased. When a fire broke out along Misakicho-dori at 2 a.m. on the morning of February 20, buildings on four sides flared up. Within seconds, a shower of sparks fell on the wooden shops and houses to the southeast. Thirty minutes later, despite desperate efforts by fire brigades belonging to local police units, the fire had spread to the adjacent districts of Jimbocho and Sarugakucho, razing schools, public buildings, halls, and hotels. All the popular stores along the streets of Nishikicho and Ogawamachi were reduced to ashes. By the time policemen and several hundred soldiers dispatched from the first division of the imperial guards had doused the last of the flames a little before 8 a.m., more than 1,500 homes were in ruins. It didn't take long for commercial instincts to reassert themselves. Vendors of celluloid glasses were heard regaling passersby with the cry, "Best spectacles to protect eyes from dust—three *sen*, only three *sen*!"

Disaster planning, modernization, and the increase in automobiles influenced the decision to widen the Ginza roadway in 1921. The willow trees that had lent grace notes to the street were cut down, and two years later the road was paved with wooden blocks held in position with asphalt and bitumen. No one at the time seems to have considered the incendiary qualities of asphalt and timber, a combination that would cause the road to ignite into a terrifying, freestanding wall of fire.

At precisely 11:58 a.m. on Saturday, September 1, 1923, Jiji news agency reporter Oshima Noburo heard what he would later describe as a noise resembling "a distant detonation." Residents were just beginning to heat cooking stoves and charcoal-burning braziers in preparation for the midday meal. The timing on this hot, windy day could not have been worse. Within one minute of striking, the 7.9 magnitude Great Kanto Earthquake, known in Japanese as the Kanto Dai Shinsai, had leveled two-thirds of Tokyo and left barely a fifth of adjacent, highly populated Yokohama standing. A second shock struck 24 hours later, followed by hundreds of minor aftershocks. The official toll numbered the fires that broke out after the quake at 134, but there were surely more.

Twenty-three-year-old Crown Prince Hirohito was having lunch at the Akasaka Palace at the time. From the safety of the palace gardens, the prince watched as black columns of smoke rose from the fires. Whether he was ever made privy to the discovery is not known, but builders at the Imperial Palace, tasked with reconstructing damaged sections of the old castle fortifications in the aftermath of the earthquake, would come across a number of skeletons standing erect within the walls. Known as *hito bashira* ("pillar men"), the gruesome sight, adding to the already phantasmagoric character of the city, recalled an ancient custom whereby human sacrifices were incarcerated within river embankments, bridges, and castles in the belief that such offerings would appease the gods and reinforce the structures.

One-room factories and wooden homes in crowded alleys, many of them with mattresses hung outside, acted as kindling for the flames that engulfed these crowded, impoverished residential zones. Approximately 400,000 buildings were destroyed, and some 63 percent of Tokyo's population was made homeless.

The extensive fires caused winds and cyclones that drove conflagrations at a speed of 800 meters per second. Ninety percent of the downtown area and 44 percent of the total area of the city were burnt down.

Tokyo was burning on both sides of the river. Bridges like those at Ryogoku and Azumabashi were crowded with people, though few could escape; the spans were burning at both ends. The writer Funaki Yoshie recalled showers of sparks falling on people standing on the decks of vessels, their hair alight, recalling an image of the fire god Fudo. A worse firestorm was at the Military Clothing Depot in the eastern district of Honjo, where crowds seeking refuge at the twenty-acre location had carried large quantities of clothes, luggage, and furniture. While the crowds settled down on this open expanse believed to act as a firebreak, a strange phenomenon was taking place as fires in the Nihonbashi commercial district merged, then leapt across the river. A similar occurrence took place as the flames from Asakusa crossed the river and combined with conflagrations in Honjo. The merging of independent fires created intensely heated vacuums to form between and above the conflagrations. The resulting wind sucked the two fires together, creating a super-inflamed cyclone that incinerated everything in its path. Those not lifted up by the spirals of flame and then dropped to the ground in molten balls of fire were caught under showers of falling sparks that set their belongings ablaze. Some 44,000 people perished at the depot. The bodies, reduced to ashes, were placed in crude receptacles made from corrugated iron.

Official figures put the number of dead and missing at 104,619, with 52,074 injured and 43,000 people reported missing. Seventy-three percent of the houses in Tokyo were damaged and 63 percent totally destroyed, along with 3,633 Buddhist temples and 151 Shinto shrines. More than 200 Christian churches had met the same fate. From the hills of Ueno Park, the imperial capital resembled an extinct city.

Open spaces were sought out as refugee camps, with tens of thousands of people occupying Hibiya and Shiba parks. Expediency trumped protocol, with thousands of homeless people camped in the grounds of Meiji Shrine, the detached palace at Hama, and in the imperial gardens at Shinjuku. The open spaces outside the Imperial Palace were quickly requisitioned, the new occupants, faced with hygiene issues, resorting to bathing in the palace moat and drying their washing on the pine trees facing the emperor's residence. The young regent, Hirohito, acquitted himself well during the emergency, donating funds to earthquake victims. He postponed plans for his own wedding, scheduled for November, and expressed his sympathy for the victims in numerous rescripts.

Newspapers quickly seized on the disaster as the most consuming story in years, one that would multiply their circulation figures. Fanning the flames of distress were unsubstantiated news reports, rumors, and speculation. Based on a series of malicious untruths, Koreans were implicated in starting fires, looting private property, poisoning wells, and inspiring acts of political sedition. The hatred was stoked at the official level by Goto Fumio, an official at the Home Ministry, who cabled police officers and ordered them to round up Koreans said to be committing acts of arson. The right-leaning *Hokkai Times* newspaper incited more fear with similar reports. One rumor claimed that 2,000 Koreans were engaged in combat with government troops, and that an army of Koreans was approaching the outskirts of Tokyo.

Koreans were convenient scapegoats, and were easily sought out in the slums where they lived by members of the police force, the notorious Black Dragon Society, military sports clubs, or anyone with a personal grudge or score to settle. Neighborhood vigilante groups, armed with bamboo spears, iron pipes, clubs and swords, were hastily formed. These Japanese volunteers, lacking rational judgment or orderly deportment, dragged Koreans from their homes and workplaces and hacked them to death. Others were strung up on telegraph poles or boiled alive in oil drums. Those who failed impromptu linguistic tests in Japanese were sentenced in mock trials and then beheaded.

The police took advantage of the hysteria to round up—and in some cases murder—socialists, labor organizers, and communists in a sweep to eliminate left-wing dissent. Trade-union polemicist Hirasawa Keishichi and nine other socialists were taken to the Kameido police station and put to death. The radical Sakae Osugi and his common-law wife, the feminist editor and agitator Ito Noe, and Ito's six-year-old nephew suffered a similar fate. They were brought in for questioning, and at a later point were strangled in their cells by a police officer who considered them to be acting against the interests of the state. Unofficial estimates put the number of massacred Koreans and activists as high as 6,000. After almost a week, the authorities stepped in to halt the bloodletting. Only a handful of prosecutions resulted from the massacres.

The 1923 disaster was an extraordinarily well-documented event, with eyewitnesses writing up their accounts in diaries, newspapers, magazines, and lithographic prints, or immortalizing the horrors in popular songs. Postcards functioned as social commentary and visual documentation. It is still possible to come across harrowing images of bodies floating in canals and ditches, or heaped into mounds that resemble Hindu funeral pyres. Other cards depict ruined buildings, panic-stricken citizens fleeing the fires, makeshift barracks housing—even the capture of an elephant that had escaped from an entertainment park in Asakusa. If some of the cards were in questionable taste, what are we to make of the reemergence of that popular Edo-period board game *sugoroku*, adapted in this instance to feature scenes from the quake? This item, which went on sale in 1924, depicted distressed refugees, camp hospitals, and firestorms on the rectangles of the board. In one particular move around the board, players advance to an illustrated panel showing survivors carrying a corpse.

The film director Kurosawa Akira described being led through the carnage by his elder brother, and seeing "piles of corpses forming little mountains. On top of one of these mountains sat a blackened body in the lotus position of Zen meditation." Kawabata Yasunari depicted the distraught survivors of the entertainment district of Asakusa rather more poetically, likening them to "a disordered field of flowers." He was accompanied on a perambulation through the ruins and around the vicinity of a pond by the writer Akutagawa Ryunosuke, whose interest in the ghoulish was well known. Akutagawa wrote rather more realistically of the scene, asking his readers to "imagine tens and hundreds of men and women as if boiled in a cauldron of mud. Muddy red cloth was strewn all up and down the banks, for most of the corpses were courtesans." Ponds, canals, and rivers had afforded little relief from the intense heat of the conflagration, which, sucking oxygen from the air, caused these water spaces to boil. Those passing Asakusa's irreparably damaged Ryounkaku caught sight of a caged monkey sitting on the site where, just a few days earlier, a circus had performed. The stunned, vacant expression on its face mirrored that of many survivors.

Aside from the loss of life, huge numbers of buildings were reduced to rubble, train tracks and tramcar lines buckled or melted, bridges were left in ruins, telegraph wires were severed, and sewer and water pipes cracked open. One building that famously survived the quake was Frank Lloyd Wright's newly completed Imperial Hotel. Though the faintly Mayan-style building's lights, telephones, stoves, and water-supply systems were put out of commission, the building was turned into a temporary relief center for the homeless, its catering staff dishing out Irish stew, dumplings, fish soup, and rice balls, all cooked on campfires around a still-working fire hydrant. The mezzanine balconies, billiard room, smoking rooms, and ballroom served as offices for displaced embassy staff. The survival of hotel owed much to the architect's use of short pilings, which he calculated would help the building to float free of a quake. This happened as planned; however, the earth beneath the hotel turned to liquefied mud, causing the building to sink by more than 60 centimeters. The hotel continued to descend over the next four decades until it was demolished in 1968.

Goto Shimpei, the visionary mayor whose earlier plans to reconstruct Tokyo had been scuppered by skeptics and naysayers, was appointed president of the Imperial Capital Reconstruction Agency. Goto immediately summoned Charles Beard, an American political scientist, urbanologist, and town-planning specialist, to lend his expertise. On seeing the devastation for himself, the American noted, "Not, perhaps, since the fire which destroyed three-fourths of London in 1666 had so large a portion of a great city been wiped out."

Goto's plans now served as the basis for the work of a special group, the Reconstruction Commission, which began expanding streets and roads and modernizing the transportation system. Their work, which achieved a modicum of success in the central areas of the city, also envisaged the creation of fireproof buildings, safe limits on construction heights, and stricter zoning for residential, industrial, and commercial districts.

Goto, who never thought in half-measures, came up with a plan to buy out the entire area affected by the quake, which, at a cost of 4.08 billion yen, was three times as large as the national budget. It was the only real master plan for rebuilding the city, but like so many before and after, it was made ineffective by party interests and the objections of landowners. The quake exposed the deficiencies of Japan's highly bureaucratized, semi-oligarchic state structure, which precluded the notion that its power elites could work together for a common cause. Roughly 9,000 factories were destroyed in the quake, leaving some 100,000 people unemployed. Many families and individuals had lost their entire assets. Thousands of salaried workers were told to leave the city and seek work elsewhere. One effect of the quake was to make the city more polycentric, as reconstruction displaced many Tokyo residents from the center. As the population shifted more to the west, Shibuya, Ikebukuro, and Shinjuku underwent rapid development as Western-style metropolitan sub-centers.

A 1925 survey taken in the central areas of Tokyo revealed that 67 percent of men now wore Western suits, at least during the working day, while 99 percent of women preferred to dress traditionally, in kimono. The exception may have been the *moga*, or "modern girl" phenomenon, a foretaste of the new faddishness and frippery that would become a hallmark of Tokyo social life. Defying tradition, these young women, along with their equally iconoclastically dapper *mobo* (modern boy) counterparts, embraced Western clothing, music, dance, and film with passion. The equivalent of Western flappers, *moga* sported body-hugging fashions, bobbed hair, and cloche hats, while the *mobo*, affecting a faintly louche manner, sauntered around in Oxford bags with lank hair and Harold Lloyd glasses. Their actual numbers were very small.

There was some substance to the style, flirtatiousness, and open sexuality of the modern woman, who was also a middle-class consumer thanks to the newfound ability to earn her own income and gain a modicum of independence from her family. Intellectually inclined young people met in milk bars, cafés, and the Ginza's German-style beer halls to engage in earnest discourse on Russian novels, the theories of Karl Marx, and the newly translated works of Schopenhauer and Kant. Depending on your perspective, *moga* were either the epitome of the new freethinker or harbingers of a moral and social decay.

Ginza, with its romantic back streets and glittering central promenade, was the main venue for these bright young things, who could be seen arm-in-arm with their male companions, smoking and drinking in the district's cafés, tea rooms, and bars; they also frequented more honky-tonk night life districts like Asakusa. Although they were a real enough phenomenon, one suspects they were partly a media creation, their assumed pro-miscuity likely exaggerated, their identification with screen idols like Gloria Swanson, Pola Negri, and Mary Pickford little more than a stylistic fad. The inordinately high number of double sui-cides in the 1920s and 1930s suggests the scenes of romantic love on the silver screen they tried to emulate were often thwarted by parents brought up in the sterner Meiji era.

Many young women took up employment as *jokyu*, or café waitresses, in the Ginza area, serving coffee, wine, whisky, and hot sandwiches. Some were known to supplement their incomes by providing sexual favors to customers. The Jazz Age tastes of New York and Paris had already spread to Tokyo, where cafés with names like "Mon Ami" and "L'Automne" sprang up. The Co-lombin, a *patisserie française*, boasted an eight-meter-high model of the Eiffel Tower and a ceiling painted by the rising young artist Fujita Tsuguharu. The three-story Café Europe in the Ginza was popular for sandwiches, cream puffs, and *baumkuchen*.

In 1907, the Nakamura-ya, a curry restaurant, moved from Kanda to Shinjuku. The old post town retained its reputation as a red-light district, a place where entertainers, itinerant monks and nuns, beggars, and prostitutes congregated. Although Naito Shinjuku Station opened in the spring of 1885, the catchment area was still associated with prostitution and the smell from the night soil carts that gathered there. The women were described as "stinking of manure." By the 1920s, however, the image of the station area had undergone a startling change. You could sample coffee and Russian chocolates at its cafés, buy European bread at the Tokyo Pan Bakery, or drop in for an afternoon matinee at the Art Deco Musashino Cinema. This was the age of the department store, or *depaato*. Mitsukoshi, a former dry-goods store, began the trend by selling a wider selection of more affordable items at the store it opened in Shinjuku in 1923.

Dedicated to self-gratification and temporary oblivion, Asakusa had an existential air that set it apart from the rest of the decidedly more driven city. On any given day there, you might see street performers, fortune-tellers, tigers jumping through flaming hoops, or a monkey beginning and ending each performance with a polite bow. You could look into a freak show; see a film; listen to the Lotus Sutra being chanted; enjoy a merry-go-round or carousel; sample exotic foreign dishes; watch bareback riders, bears, and elephants; take in a striptease show; or visit the sensational Panoramakan, a long wooden building, where life-size models of soldiers and wall paintings recreated scenes from the American Civil War and Japan's own more recent conflict with China. Beyond Asakusa Pond was an ill-lit area known as the Dark Quarter, which was a front for prostitution. Rows of small houses went under names like *Shinbun-juran-sho* (Newspaper Reading Hall), *Kissaten* (Tea-drinking Shop), and *Meishuya* (Drinking Shop).

Before the great earthquake foreshortened its life, the twelve-story hexagonal brick building called the Ryounkaku ("Cloud-Piercing Tower") could be seen reflected in the pond. Just below the tower might be found a late-night *gyu-ya* (beef shop) catering to laborers enjoying cheap cuts of beef, pork, and horsemeat from steaming pans set out on tables. Pickpockets and gamblers lurked amid the stinging odor of coarse sake, thick clouds of tobacco smoke, and the smell of boiling flesh. After a show, you could eat broiled eel at the Yakko, just behind the Higashi Hongan-ji temple; sample snapping turtles at the Jubako in Sanya; try the horsemeat at the Okada in Hatchobori; or have pan-simmered clams at one of the little eating houses situated on the floor below the Shinagawa brothels.

The area's first film house, the Denkikan, or Electric Hall, opened in the entertainment block known as the Rokko in 1903. Scenes from Kabuki and *chambara* (Japanese sword-fighting dramas) were still immensely popular, but you could also see Robert Wiene's 1919 film *The Cabinet of Doctor Caligari*, and experimental works by Japanese directors, like Thomas Kurihara's *The Lasciviousness of the Viper*, or *A Page Out of Order*, a disturbing

Expressionist film by Kinugasa Teinosuke. Among the billboards depicting popular Japanese actors were the faces of Lionel Barrymore, Gloria Swanson, and Douglas Fairbanks. The Marx Brothers' *Duck Soup* was a box-office hit, though the Japanese title—in emulation of Soseki Natsume's famous novel *I Am a Cat*—was changed to *I Am a Duck*. The Asakusa Enoken's Casino Folie, a revue where scantily-clad women kicked up their legs in so-called "opera" performances, opened in 1929.

Hedonism, the search for immersion or self-oblivion, belied the underlying poverty of districts like Asakusa. If you peered under the floor of Senso-ji temple's great veranda at almost any time of the day or night, you could spot men, women, and children in deep sleep, either huddled together for warmth or stretched out on threadbare reed mats. These were the beggars and outcasts of the district, of whom the younger and more streetwise might be recruited as apprentices by pickpockets.

Given the levels of social inequality, the rise of more assertive proletariat movements was inevitable. "Taisho democracy" was a term coined by post–World War II Japanese historians to describe a period of social unrest and change in matters of education, culture, and media participation. The period saw the formation of unions to protect workers' rights, the questioning of women's traditional roles, a relaxing of censorship and government surveillance, and the introduction of modest steps towards parliamentary procedure.

This Taisho breed of democracy, however, was rather different from the West's: more a version of populism in which the function of government was to promote welfare, and in which policy-making was based on national will within the context of an imperial system. The economic downturn after the First World War had led to more labor disputes and increasing social unrest. Riots protesting increases in the price of rice broke out throughout the country in 1918. Social tensions rose with the violent suppression of the riots, but so, too, did hopes among

Japanese socialists and communists that great change modeled on the Bolshevik Revolution might be at hand. A mass rally organized by the newly politicized "silent majority" took place in Hibiya Park in 1919, its aim the granting of universal suffrage without discrimination.

The so-called "new woman" of the Meiji era was now demanding a good deal more than state welfare to support families. Discussions of female suffrage, freedom of education, economic opportunities and equality, independence, and the right to individuality, however, were confined almost exclusively to urban areas like Tokyo. Here, an increasing number of middle-class women entered the workplace in the 1920s, taking jobs as department store clerks, government functionaries, nurses, telephone operators, beauticians, nurses, typists, café waitresses, teachers, storekeepers, chauffeurs, bus conductors, gasoline girls, and writers. It is plausible that the sexual harassment of women riding Tokyo's electric trains was a reaction to the idea that working females represented a radical departure from their assigned role as wives and mothers. The molestation was, therefore, justified—the reasoning went—as any working female must be a woman of loose or questionable virtue.

Pitched battles between workers at the Kyodo Printing Company in Koishikawa took place in January 1926 after the firm dismissed print workers who had gone on strike over enforced part-time work. Strikes by female bus and train conductors increased in the late 1920s and 1930s as the economy contracted. Incensed at a plan to cut wages and reduce monthly holidays from five to three, five hundred women conductors employed by the Tokyo Municipal Bus Company staged a strike in July 1928.

Crude methods were used to deal with dissent: the services of mobsters were enlisted alongside the police force when strikes needed to be broken, or protesters were to be brought to their knees. When young women at the Toyo Muslin, a major textile plant in the eastern neighborhood of Kameido, staged a protest after being summarily dismissed for objecting to dismal working conditions, a number of sympathetic local residents joined in. The protest, which occurred in 1930, was swiftly put down by the police with the aid of hired thugs. The erosion of any gains women had made in the 1920s was evident a decade later, as the authorities simultaneously began rounding up female activists while eulogizing women who they saw as models of motherhood, thrift, and self-abnegation.

The short-lived freedoms that characterized the Taisho era have been compared to the liberating excesses of Weimar-era Berlin. The frivolities of the 1920s Tokyo were one thing, but dissidence was another. The revised aim of Japan under the command of new leaders and a compliant military eager to discredit the gains of the Taisho era was to be modern without being democratic. A change in mood was soon evident even in entertainment districts like Asakusa, where the jitterbug, the shimmy, and the beguine were replaced by the serried thump of military boots as people took up new melodies like *The Imperial Army Marches Off* and *Military Spy Song*. Revue audiences were now treated to such edifying productions as the *Decisive Aerial Warfare Suite*. In retrospect, the authorial tolerance of the preceding era appears more like a lapse of attention concealing the massing of darker intentions.

The death of the Taisho emperor in 1926 and the enthronement of his son, Hirohito, was a national media event. The unity of subjects and monarch, ancestors with the living, ritual with governance, was officially sealed on the morning of November 15, 1928, when, having passed the night in the presence of the sun goddess Amaterasu Omikami at the sacred shrines at Ise, the new emperor was formally transfigured into a living god. On his return to Tokyo, he could be seen decked out in full military uniform, reviewing some 35,000 marching troops. He then proceeded to the naval dock, where the imperial gaze of approval was cast over 208 ships, two aircraft carriers, and thirty-nine recently commissioned submarines. The period of Hirohito's reign was subsequently dubbed Showa, the age of "Illustrious peace."

The writer Akutagawa Ryunosuke, a leading figure of the age, would take poison in the first year of the new imperial reign. His suicide note spoke of an "obscure sense of anxiety about the future," a sentiment shared by many intellectuals of the day. As the Japanese readied to enter the *kuraitani*, the "dark valley," as it would come to be known, Akutagawa's vaguely sensed unease would acquire the ominous actuality of premonition.

Despite its seclusion, Tokyo's Imperial Palace is little more than a stone's throw away from the business of daily life. Originally completed on the grounds of Edo Castle in 1889, many of its key structures were destroyed in an air raid in 1945 and were subsequently rebuilt. (Dreamstime © Haveseen)

CHAPTER 5

Hachiman, God of War

Assassinations – Censorship – A failed coup –
Mobilizing for war – Air raids

Construction of a new Diet building, home to the Upper and Lower Houses, was completed at a staggering cost of 26 million yen in the autumn of 1936, just in time for the seventieth session of parliament convened for that winter. The structure represented an earnest, nationalist-inspired effort to have a building made by Japanese architects, with Japanese materials and labor.

Apart from the pneumatic carriers and locks, thermostatic heaters, and mail chutes—which were imported from the United States—and a number of stained-glass windows and mirrors from England, the building was an entirely Japanese enterprise. The designers and contractors of the steel-framed structure, which was set in concrete, with a liberal tonnage of marble on the inside and granite on the exterior, claimed the building was indestructible, even in a major earthquake. The Diet building still stands today, vindicating their confidence. Its 65.8-meter tower was the highest point in the city at the time, but because it overlooked the Imperial Palace grounds, the public was not permitted to take in the view, which would have been an unthinkable impertinence.

The decade witnessed Tokyo transformed in other ways, as it

became the center for the foremost concentration of heavy industry in the country. The headquarters of almost all the most prominent private financial enterprises in Japan were to be found here, making it by far the most advanced industrialized capital in Asia. The city's boundaries were redrawn in the 1920s and again in 1932, absorbing contingent towns and villages and consolidating them into twenty new wards to make a total of thirty-five in the city. Greater Tokyo could now boast a population of 4,970,000, making it the second-largest city in the world after New York. The technical classification of Tokyo as a city would change in 1943, however, by combining Tokyo Prefecture and the existing city into *Tokyo-to*, the Tokyo Metropolis. The administrative reach of this new entity included land masses far to the south of the city, such as the Izu Islands and the Ogasawara Islands—the latter being a twenty-six-hour boat ride from Tokyo Bay.

The skies expanded as well, with the completion of Haneda Airport in 1931. The new Tsukiji marketplace, destined to become the largest wholesale market in the world, opened for business in February of 1935. Its first sales were of fresh-caught fish, produce, and poultry; sales of dried and salted fish began in June. The playwright Osanai Kaoru, back in Tokyo after study trips to Russia and Germany, built the 1924 Tsukiji Little Theater near the market, just a few blocks from the Kabuki-za. Here he produced plays by Chekhov, Shaw, Ibsen, and other heavyweight Western dramatists, which attracted a small, mostly young audience of students and High City intellectuals.

A new temple was built in Tsukiji that seemed to embody the emerging imperial Pan-Asian aspirations of the day. Constructed in reinforced concrete, the Tsukiji Hongan-ji temple opened in 1934. Signs of post-earthquake modernization were not apparent to everyone. The British writer Peter Quennell, who much preferred the reassuring geomantic unities of the Chinese capital, described Tokyo in his 1932 book, *A Superficial Journey through Tokyo and Peking*, as follows:

Vague and slatternly, a sprawling skyline of wooden
houses overlooked by a massive procession of telegraph poles linked together by loose wires in a droop-
ing curve...they lurch drunkenly over the cowering
shabby roofs and lean at affected angles on strong sup-
ports. The old Japan is changing in their shadow; the
future belongs to them and all they symbolize.

Even in 1935, the Ginza's Tokyo Café Sabo was still opening its
Summer Beer Salon to customers as usual. By 1940, however, the
coffeehouses and bars were half-empty, the result of an unofficial,
self-imposed ban on pleasure, which was now construed to be un-
patriotic. This was a most unwelcome development to the writer
Nagai Kafu, a frequent customer at the coffee shops of Ginza
and the backrooms of Asakusa revues. An unapologetic senti-
mentalist, always an era out of step with the times, the Showa era
inspired in him a predictable longing for Taisho times. First published in book form in 1937, his story *Bokuto kidan* (A Strange
Tale from East of the River) is set in the working-class red light
quarter of Tamanoi (present-day Higashi-Mukojima). Unlike the
works of young Meiji-era novelist Higuchi Ichiyo, whose prostitutes were symbols of failure and penury, Kafu's women, like his
nostalgia-soaked writing, were reminders of a lost age. Even the
dereliction of an area like Tamanoi, with its pestilential canals,
tainted by the industrial filth from nearby smokestacks, could stir
his poetic longing. Describing his central character, O-Yuki, he
wrote, "Her hair always in one of the old styles, and the foulness
of the canal, and the humming of the mosquitoes—all of these
stirred me deeply, and called up visions of a past now dead some
thirty or forty years." The work was not banned, but was frowned
upon by the authorities for its failure to support the war effort.

The airwaves, once full of popular songs, now played host to
an increasing fare of military songs with plenty of muscular brass,

mournful violas, and strangulated, propagandist tirades, which replaced radio melodies. Filmmaking was undergoing a similar revision of taste and content. The filmmaker Ozu Yasujiro pursued his examination of socioeconomic conditions by showing Depression-hit Japan in his 1935 film *Tokyo no Yado* (An Inn in Tokyo), one of his most moving pictures. A father and his young son trudge the back streets of Tokyo vainly seeking work and, with few possessions, must choose between food and shelter. In an era of growing surveillance, funding for such films, even seemingly innocuous foreign imports, would be impossible. Films like Raoul Walsh's *The Thief of Bagdad* were soon replaced with stirring Japanese titles like *Fatherland, Mud and Soldiers, Song of the Advancing Army,* and *The Story of Tank Commander Nishizumi.*

The requisitioning of entertainment by the authorities was evident in its approach to Kabuki. The government, eager to promote models of loyalty and patriotism that would serve the war effort, attempted to propagandize the form, commissioning heavily censored new plays like the 1932 *Three Heroic Human Bombs,* and *Kojiki,* a 1940 work featuring Japan's mythological Sun Goddess, Amaterasu, who in her new role was tasked with benignly casting the light of civilization over Asia, or at least those Asian nations under the heel of Japan's imperium.

On November 4, 1921, Hara Takashi, prime minister and leader of the Freedom Party, was knifed to death while standing on a platform at Tokyo Station; the incident signaled an open season for assassinations of political figures. Blaming political parties and the moneyed elite for the economic malaise gripping Japan after World War I, three radical right-wing groups emerged. Members of the Blood Oath League, headed by a fanatic follower of the Buddhist Nichiren sect, swore to assassinate one notable politician or financier each. In February 1932, a member of the group shot dead former finance minister Inoue Junnosuke. Dan Takuma, head of the powerful Mitsui Financial group, met the same fate the following month.

In a curious footnote to the times, a plan hatched by a group of far rightists to assassinate Charlie Chaplin was a measure of how far things had gone. The director was hugely popular in Japan. *City Lights* had just been released and his arrival in Japan in 1932 was greeted with adulation. The Meiji Confectionary Company even released a hugely profitable line of Chaplin Caramels. But Chaplin noticed his hosts behaving strangely. As his car drove past the Imperial Palace, for example, it came to a halt, and he was asked to step out of the limousine and bow toward the emperor's residence, even though no officials were present. Chaplin's party was also threatened at a restaurant that evening.

The following day, May 15, as Chaplin was attending a sumo-wrestling match with the son of Prime Minister Inukai Tsuyoshi, an outspoken liberal who had campaigned for parliamentary democracy, the young man was called away by an attendant and informed that his father had been assassinated by a group of nine naval cadets. It transpired that Chaplin had also been an intended target in the spate of killings, which was supposed to create confusion to coincide with a planned *coup d'etat* by a clique calling themselves the Ketsumeidan, or "Blood Brotherhood."

Henry Pu Yi, the hapless last emperor of China's Qing dynasty, who was also Japan's puppet ruler over its colony of Manchuria, visited Tokyo at this time. Manchuria under the Japanese was supposed to be both the industrial foundry and farmland of the empire, and for a time it was. If the agony of one people can provision the banquet table of another, Japan's northern colony did so. It should be remembered, however, that Japan's wartime incursions were not, for the most part, into free and sovereign countries, but colonial possessions, foreign concessions, and settlements dominated by Westerners whose sense of racial supremacy was not questioned.

A handful of Japanese genuinely believed in a liberation doctrine—the freeing of the continent from the grip of Western colonial powers, the stirring rhetoric of the so-called Greater East

Asia Co-Prosperity Sphere—even as Japan's armies were swarming mercilessly across China. The air of entitlement the Japanese subsequently cultivated was not so different from that evinced by the British, French, and other Westerners, whom they merely imitated in their colonial practices and mannerisms, and then eventually supplanted. With Japan's fortunes improving in Asia, powerful men, generals, and industrialists turned into saturnine monsters, overwhelming the good intentions of progressive reformists at home.

The most serious armed insurrection the nation had seen in a very long time took place a little before dawn on February 26, 1936. With dense snow covering the city, more than 2,000 Tokyo-based troops aligned with the Kodo-ha (Imperial Way) faction staged a coup d'état known as the Ni-Ni-Roku Jiken, or "2-26 Incident," with the avowed intention of establishing a Showa Restoration. Disgruntled with political corruption and cuts in military funding, many of the enlisted men were from the rural northeast of the country, a region where hardship was common.

Key politicians, including military and civil officials, were targeted for assassination, important buildings in the city center earmarked for occupation. Residents who owned radios listened nervously for news. Most of it was bad: the inspector-general of military education was assassinated, as was the lord keeper of the privy seal. Finance Minister Takahashi Korekiyo, a moderate who had initiated a program of fiscal cutbacks on military spending, was shot seven times, and then, for good measure, dispatched with one sword blow, administered diagonally in the samurai style. The prime minister, Admiral Okada Keisuke, narrowly escaped death. To his credit, the emperor acted with alacrity, ordering his army minister to "suppress the rebels within one hour." By February 29, with the army confronting the insurgents and naval warships amassed in Tokyo Bay, the coup had lost most of its steam; the troops returned to their barracks and the conspirators were branded as mutineers. The incident was another example of the military insubordination that Emperor Meiji had noted when he complained, "The army seems to have a tendency to be difficult to lead."

The poet and philosopher Rabindranath Tagore visited Tokyo for the fourth time in 1929. The warm welcome he received from government officials and admirers quickly wore off as his loathing for Japanese militarism and aggression in China became clear. In a 1938 letter to the poet Noguchi Yone, an apologist for Japan's ambitions in Asia, Tagore would express his "utter sorrow" at developments on the continent, writing with astonishing prescience,

> I know that one day the disillusionment of your people will be complete, and through laborious centuries they will have to clear the debris of their civilization wrought to ruin by their own warlords run amok. They will realize that the aggressive war on China is insignificant as compared to the destruction of the inner spirit of chivalry of Japan, which is proceeding with a ferocious severity.

By that time, the *kenpeitai* (military police) were dealing swiftly and harshly with real and potential opposition wherever they found it. Yanaihara Tadao, a prominent scholar of colonial politics and a pacifist, was expelled from his post at Tokyo Imperial University in 1937 on the grounds of his anti-militarist stance. Other educators, intellectuals, and freethinkers were extirpated and replaced with a new breed of patriot. After two failed coups, sporadic assassinations, the escalation of war in China, labor shortages, and difficulties in procuring military supplies, the mood in Tokyo was tense. With government campaigns and slogans like "All-Out Spiritual Mobilization," the rationing of everyday articles, and the setting up of neighborhood associations tasked with spying on local residents, the military stood one step closer to establishing a totalitarian state.

Visits to shrines dedicated to Hachiman, the god of war, were especially popular. Religion flourished, as it often does in times of uncertainty, with the conviction that the conflict would be a sacred war. Shinto rituals were used to provide a spiritual endorsement for militarism in much the same way that Christianity and Islam had requisitioned a higher authority to empower their crusades and other holy causes. Devout Buddhists—those who took the Buddha's teachings of compassion to heart—withheld their support for Japan's fifteen-year period of militarism in the Asia-Pacific region, withdrawing into an ecclesiastical silence, but several religious groups, such as the Kokuchukai (National Pillar Association), threw their lot in with the military, preaching an aggressive brand of armed patriotism. Emperor Meiji's fondness for the army had caused him to indulge his commanders, imposing little control over their actions in the field—an attitude that played right into the hands of his grandson's bellicose and far more ambitious generals.

Once the emperor had determined that war was inevitable, he bent with the wind. Though he may have harbored a personal disinclination for armed conflict, the emperor was a nationalist before being a pacifist, and had no intention of seeing his empire dismantled by an American embargo on oil imports to Japan. Although he opposed the war until November of 1941, and had confronted military leaders about the improbability of their assurances of a six-month victory in the Pacific, once the die was cast, there was no going back. Fully briefed with plans for the attack on Pearl Harbor, he was also well informed about strategies for the military incursions that took place throughout Southeast Asia and the subsequent battles that would rage in the South Pacific and Okinawa.

Not everyone was keen to make the sacrifice and go to the front line. Prohibitions on tattooing were introduced during the war as a response to an increasing number of young men seeking ways to avoid conscription. People wearing tattoos were considered nonconformists who might spread dissent among the military ranks. Open opposition to the war meant immediate incarceration or worse. There were some well-known figures, however, whose silent objections were clear. Nagai Kafu refused to write anything during the war in order to demonstrate his refusal to support it, earning praise after the conflict finally ended and the country's postwar pacifist phase began. He did keep a diary during the war years, though. "Let their crimes be recorded for eternity," he wrote of the militarists in 1944; and, more hopefully, "However cruel and arbitrary the methods of the government may be, they cannot restrain the imagination. While there is life, there will be freedom." The only official action that Nagai, a lover of shadows and moods, appears to have approved of was the ban on neon signs. He recorded his thoughts on strolling toward Asakusa's opera house in the evening thus: "There being no neon, the moon lit the tall buildings...The prohibition against neon signs must be described as an enlightened act by our unenlightened military government." Once the gloves were off, conventional warfare turned into a battle of total annihilation. Gripped by a passionate ignorance of the inevitable outcome of war, Japan slipped inexorably into poverty, shortages, and hardship.

Nineteen forty-one was the Year of the Snake; on December 7, the emperor, dressed in a naval uniform, was informed that Japanese dive-bombers and torpedoes had destroyed the greater part of the US fleet at Pearl Harbor. On hearing of the success of the operation, palace officials noted in their diaries and official records, "His Majesty was in an exceedingly good mood." The respected literary critic Takao Okuna captured the euphoria sweeping the country when he wrote, "We Japanese had never in our entire history, felt such pride in our race as we did at that moment."

With little effective military resistance to its expansion in Asia, the war was going well for Japan. Robert Guillain, a French journalist who visited Japan in 1938 and found himself obliged to stay in the capital after the outbreak of hostilities, recalled the jubilant atmosphere in the city and among its inhabitants in 1942:

> Evenings in Tokyo were an Oriental carnival…In the narrow streets, fittingly darkened by the blackout, almost all the passers-by entering or leaving the restaurants were either tight or tipsy. They staggered, bawled patriotic songs in staccato rhythms, dragged their wooden sandals and scuffed shoes dreadfully as they zigzagged from bar to bar.

The first experimental air raid on Tokyo occurred on April 18, 1942, when a squadron of sixteen B25s was launched from the aircraft carrier *USS Hornet*. Although the damage to a steel mill, an oil tank, a farm, a number of small power plants, and civilian sites such as schools and an army hospital was minimal, and only thirty-nine casualties were recorded, the sortie, known as the Doolittle Raid, proved the point that Tokyo was no longer invulnerable from the air. The United States, armed to the teeth with the world's most advanced military technology, now had Tokyo in its crosshairs.

Despite increasing food shortages, unconfirmed rumors of defeats in the Pacific, and the ever more common sight of relatives at funerals holding white urns containing the remains of sons fallen in battle, spirits were still high. The personal losses were stoically accepted as a necessary sacrifice for the greater good of the nation. A belief in the invincibility of Japan was captured in a poem that Japanese schoolchildren were required to memorize: "Our great Japan, whose emperor is a descendant of God. Our nation has never lost to its enemies. Daily the country shines more brightly with glory." During the Meiji era, Buddhist temples, government offices, schools, and other public buildings had been urged to replace their old wooden gates with more contemporary wrought- and cast-iron ones; many of these were taken up in the drive to collect scrap metal for the war effort. Sentimentality, however, could still survive in the traumatized city. Though it had been dismantled for its bronze parts, the crane fountain in Hibiya Park, a fond remnant of the Meiji era, was spared and eventually reassembled.

The Tokyo air raids snapped people out of their delirium. The mood was heavy with foreboding in the long, dry summer of 1944. Dust piled up in drifts on rooftops as scorching winds blew through the city. If its citizens seemed listless, malnutrition accounted for some of the apathy. Many shops were closed for business. Long lines formed in front of food stores as volunteers dug roadside air-raid trenches that only added more dust to the air.

As the raids continued, gallows humor took over, with residents naming the American planes *okyakusama* (honorable guests), and "regular mail." The haiku master Kato Shuson, who experienced the air raids firsthand, wrote in one poem:

In the depths of fire
Seeing the way
A peony crumbles

This haiku came from Kato's experience of witnessing his own house destroyed and his wife and children separated. One interpretation of the verse is that the way a wooden frame house buckles and disintegrates under flames is similar to the way the petals of a peony wither and then fall. Historian John Dower wrote, "Atrocities follow war as the jackal follows a wounded beast." Japan was that cornered animal, now at the mercy of a formidable and vindictive enemy. Air raids by Superfortress B-29s over Tokyo began in earnest in November 1944.

An air raid on January 27, 1945, left roughly 1,000 civilians dead in the Ginza district. There were so many corpses in nearby Hibiya Park that stray dogs were killed to prevent them from consuming the bodies. A major shift in the intensity of the raids occurred on the night of March 9, 1945, when indiscriminate carpet bombing and nighttime raids began. Military strategy had changed, with the Americans now bent on causing mass casualties to civilian populations as they later would with Hiroshima and Nagasaki. In order to hasten an end to the war by setting the city on fire, high-explosive bombs used to take out individual buildings were replaced by B-29 Superfortress bombers loaded with as much as six tons of a new incendiary substance called napalm (later to be used extensively in a different Asian battle zone). The main target of the new mix of jellied gasoline and magnesium was the high-density area of Asakusa ward, where narrow lanes and alleys and a profusion of flammable roofs would extract a maximum death toll. The authorities instructed residents to dig their own air-raid shelters consisting of holes in the ground covered with tatami mats soaked in water, which became, in the event, little more than fiery tombs. In a three-hour period from midnight to 3 a.m., 334 bombers dropped a total of 1,700 tons of incendiaries on the city. Between eighty and a hundred thousand civilians perished that night, the single most destructive bombing mission in military history. It was the first of America's high-tech massacres.

As the incendiary bombs exploded and the fires spread, the sky was so bright that US airmen could reportedly read the dials on their watches even at an altitude of 20,000 feet. The bombing created a firestorm that reached speeds of up to 112 kph and temperatures of 1,000 degrees Celsius. The architect of this sickening carnage, General Curtis LeMay, would later confess that, had America been defeated, he would have been tried as a war criminal for the civilians that, as he said in his own words, he had "scorched, boiled, and baked to death."

Women wrapped bundles of cloth around their heads to avoid choking in the fumes, but many of these caught fire. For a few terrible hours the fierce combustion sucked much of the oxygen out of the city. In what Radio Tokyo referred to as a program of "slaughter bombings," heat from the raids caused metal to melt, canals to boil, and human beings to burst into flames. It would take twenty-five days to remove the dead from the ruins. In the superheated atmosphere of war, American citizens could perhaps be forgiven for not expressing remorse at the victims of the Tokyo raids. After all, the Japanese themselves had set a high bar for indifference toward civilians with their terror bombings of Chongqing as early as 1938—raids specifically targeted at residential areas, resulting in the incineration of tens of thousands of Chinese civilians.

With bombs raining down on Tokyo, food, fuel, and shelter were in desperately short supply. Like the laborers of Leningrad who had been forced to boil their leather belts to make soup during the German bombardment of 1941, many families in Tokyo, reduced to a diet of sweet potatoes, were obliged to cut down wooden telephone poles for heating fuel. In such circumstances, it was becoming increasingly difficult for the government to convince people that they were still winning the war, that a supreme victory was just a matter of time. Bombs were even reaching the inner sanctum of mystical patriotism—key buildings within the grounds of the Imperial Palace were destroyed in early 1945.

The Japanese, knowing that everything is provisional, that cities are replaceable, were less distressed about the physical condition of Tokyo than the immediate means of survival. Upon being discharged from a Tokyo hospital where he had received treatment for injuries after being shot down, Sakai Saburo, one of the Japan's most decorated fighter pilots, described the feeling of disillusionment and resentment at the way the war was being conducted, and the attitude of civilians to men who had not perished at sea or on the battlefields of Asia:

> Street-corner radios were blasting war songs and broadcasting news of fake victories...passengers on the train I took, especially the young girls and women,

only glanced my way one time, grimacing at my appearance, then looking the other way. Their determination to avoid looking at my bloodstained bandages unnerved and angered me. No longer was I a leading pilot, but a bloodied, filthy, and distasteful sight to my own people.

On May 25, the late-spring skies were full of clouds, illuminated from beneath by red flames and a forest of searchlight beams. The duralumin coating of the fuselages of enemy planes, poised on the pedestals of these pillars of light, turned violet as the little-remembered Great Yamanote Air Raid, an attack on residential districts that included Nakano, Azabu, Shibuya, and Akasaka, commenced. This final air raid on Tokyo's urban areas claimed the lives of more than 3,600 civilians.

The city was in agony, but observers at a safe distance could, on occasion, wax lyrical about the air raids. Novelist and essayist Takeyama Michio described the central pool of light where the planes entered as "a red lotus of fire." The beauty of writings like this is perplexing, but Takeyama explains: "In those air-raid days, each new day, we thought, was 'the end of the world.' It was a shock to see that the end of the world was so beautiful, like the hallucinations of a lunatic."

Robert Guillain, the French journalist for *Le Monde*, had little choice but to watch the incineration, writing:

> Tokyo, which had never been a beautiful city, had now become a dirty city. The capital woke up each morning a little more sordid, as if tainted by the doom-laden night in which it had bathed. The raids had still to begin, and yet, night after night, an obsession gripped the city plunged into darkness by the blackout.

Well aware of the vulnerability of a city constructed largely of flammable materials, Guillain added, "Tokyo was a giant village of wooden boards, and it knew it."

Another foreigner who found himself in the wrong place at the wrong time was Raymond Halloran, a navigator-bombardier on an earlier mission in January 1945 to target the Nakajima aircraft factory in western Tokyo. Forced to abort his B-29 plane and parachute to the ground after being shot down by Japanese twin-engine fighters, Halloran was taken by the military police to a prison where he was placed in solitary confinement. The hapless American, who spent much of the remainder of his stay in a torture facility near the Imperial Palace, survived both near-starvation and the Great Tokyo Air Raid, but not the humiliation of captivity. In April, prison guards blindfolded him and tied his hands with rope. He was then taken to Ueno Zoo, where he was put on display to the public, naked, inside a tiger cage.

The Imperial Palace, a Meiji-era ensemble of buildings, was laid waste by American firebombs in June, 1945. Meiji Shrine was burned down the following day. The shogunal mausoleums at Shiba were obliterated at the same time. The psychological effect of the destruction of the imperial residence, at a time when morale was at its lowest point, can only be imagined. It was not enough, however, to deter the emperor from approving operations he believed would gain Japan a decisive victory and a stronger hand when entering into peace negotiations. The subsequent battles of the Philippines and Okinawa were catastrophic for Japan, now isolated after the surrender of its ally Germany.

Doubt in the ideology of an authoritarian state based on a national polity overseen by a sacred figurehead was surfacing in graffiti messages that began to appear on walls and lampposts, like "End the war," "Overturn the government," and "Is the emperor not a human being?" Similar messages surfaced in anonymous letters sent to newspapers. These, along with correspondence sent to the palace and newspaper companies, were never made public. After being taken on a rapid tour of the smouldering ruins of Tokyo, the emperor was upset at the lack of deference and veneration shown toward him by the thousands of numbed and homeless Tokyo citizens.

The summer of 1945 is remembered for its sizzling heat and atomic explosions. In Tokyo, the raids continued with dreadful predictability and soaring mortalities, until noon on August 15, 1945, when the emperor broadcast his announcement of surrender. The speech, in an archaic court language few Japanese could comprehend, was transmitted across the airwaves in a vocal form known as the Voice of the Crane. This referred to an imperial command whose resonance would reverberate in the sky, like that of a crane's cry, even after the bird's passing. The emperor exhorted his subjects to "bear the unbearable, endure the unendurable, and seek peace." It was a well-crafted piece of rhetoric, skillfully repositioning the Japanese as the victims rather than perpetrators of the war. The speech made no reference to Japan's own atomic bomb program, which was being developed at Tokyo University.

That night, a cabal of renegade officers burst into the office of the commander of the Imperial Guard Headquarters and shot him dead. Issuing false orders in the commander's name, the officers persuaded the guards to seize the Imperial Palace and encircle the emperor for his own protection. The coup was quelled by dawn, and the leaders dutifully committed suicide. The nightmare that cost almost three million Japanese lives, not to mention an infinitely higher number in the Asia and Pacific region, was not quite over. In order to atone for Japan's surrender, some members of the officer corps committed ritual suicide in the grounds of the Imperial Palace Outer Garden.

To many visiting the capital in the days after the surrender, the city was unrecognizable, a landscape bearing little or no resemblance to the vibrant prewar metropolis. Tokyo was no longer a functioning city, but the charred remains of a hecatomb.

The crane fountain in Unkei Pond in Hibiya Park. (Photo by Kakidai printed under the Creative Commons Attribution-Share Alike 3.0 Unported License)

Once the center of the black market in radio parts, Akihabara is now an electronics hub of a different kind. Its literally hundreds of shops for hard-and-software have earned Akihabara the nickname "Electric Town." Also considered the heart of "Otaku" culture, Akihabara abounds in manga, anime, and their fans—"cosplayers" who use costume to escape into the world of their favorite characters. (Dreamstime © Sean Pavone)

CHAPTER 6

Occupying Bodies

*US governance – Censorship – Black markets –
Tokyo Trials – Cultural resurgence*

Reduced to one massive, pulverized slum, a scorched plain, the city appeared at times to be filled with a palpable optimism—that heightened zest for life only those who have just felt the wings of death brush against them can feel. "We had lost the war, so why wasn't anybody mournful?" an ex-serviceman in a Kyogoku Natsuhiko novel asks.

> Everything we had believed in was now proven wrong. When we attacked the enemy they told us we were glorious balls of fire: when soldiers died they said it was like the breaking of jewels. The government continuously preached the justness of the national struggle, but when it was all over the attitude of our leaders changed overnight, becoming devotees of democracy, while Japanese citizens, impoverished people, appeared to be more animated than ever.

Japanese citizens, refusing to be sullen, largely embraced the *volte-face* from ultra-nationalism to the reforms being introduced by the American occupiers. They were, to quote from a panel in Yoshihiro Tatsumi's graphic novel, *A Drifting Life,* starting to see the benefits of being "finally liberated from a life of daily suffering." Filmmaker Kurosawa Akira recalled being summoned to his studio in Setagaya ward to hear the emperor's radio speech. "The owners of some shops, in readiness for the Honorable Death of the Hundred Million, had removed their prized Japanese swords from their sheaths and were sitting staring at the bare blades. When I walked home along the same route after listening to the imperial proclamation, the official surrender, people on the shopping streets looked cheerful, as if a festival was about to take place."

Despite the brave face being put on defeat, Japan was now a demoralized country: children suffered from ringworm, women sold their bodies to make ends meet, and men who thought they were serving their country were despised for the ruination they had brought down on their nation. Human dignity suffered along with the loss of life. In Ueno Park and its peripheries, the homeless built shelters and dugouts, taking over the burnt-out burial grounds and tombs of the Tokugawa shoguns. Thousands of homeless people lived in makeshift shelters or in city parks. Many froze to death in the bitter winters of 1946 and 1947, when the cold, like acid, ate through their frayed kimonos and rags. Many of the elderly, ravaged within, dressed in white overalls resembling hospital gowns. Families sold off everything they possessed in order to survive.

It became common to see Japanese veterans standing on the streets with missing limbs, hands held out with begging bowls. These flesh-and-blood specters in their tattered military fatigues were the embodiment of stories emerging under the Occupation-controlled media of suicide attacks, atrocities, cannibalism, and military failure; they represented everything Japan was trying to forget. Accordingly, they were mostly ignored, consigned to the margins inhabited by outcasts. The vilification of military leaders was, likewise, less a judgment on their moral shortcomings in waging war than on their inability to win it.

The Occupation period officially began on September 2, 1945, with the signing of surrender documents aboard the *USS Missouri*. The presiding figure for most of the period was General Douglas MacArthur, Supreme Commander for the Allied Powers (SCAP). The general made it quite clear who would be in charge going forward by having four hundred B-29 bombers and fifteen hundred US Navy fighter planes fly in close formation at the end of the ceremony, with Mount Fuji in the background. As an added touch, the flag that had been flown by Commodore Perry's black ships on his two missions to Japan almost a hundred years earlier was displayed at the surrender ceremony.

The general's arrival on Japanese soil was equally theatrical. MacArthur had touched down at Atsugi naval aerodrome near Yokohama on August 30, pausing at the top of the plane stairs just long enough for the press photographers to capture the carefully orchestrated pose, the globally syndicated image of the commander with his trademark cap, corncob pipe, and aviator sunglasses. The fact that he concealed his eyes behind darkened frames made an uncanny impression on the Japanese; in Japan, only the blind wore glasses that hid their eyes.

Many of Tokyo's choice buildings were requisitioned by the occupiers. The Allied Forces' general headquarters were located on commandingly higher floors, directly opposite the Imperial Palace, in the Daiichi Mutual Life Insurance Company building in Hibiya. The large Matsuya and Hattori stores in the Ginza were seized by the US Eighth Army and used as post-exchange stores; the Iwasaki Mansion in Yushima was requisitioned for use as administrative offices; and the elegant Tsunamachi Mitsui Club in Mita became the "GHQ Club." Large sections of the Tsukiji fish market were taken over for use as a motor pool and laundry for supplying Occupation offices and billets in the nearby districts of Marunouchi and Ginza. Rules of engagement decreed that occupiers and occupied maintain a "respectful distance," which led, at the Mimatsu Nightclub, to martinets moving around the dance floor with six-inch rulers measuring the required distance between Americans and their Japanese dancing partners. It didn't take long, given the gregarious nature of the new occupiers and the curiosity of the occupied, for this to break down.

Fearing that the "Anglo-Saxon beasts" would engage in the mass rape of Japanese womanhood, the Japanese authorities, under the auspices of the Relaxation and Amusement Association (RAA), quickly set up licensed brothels, or "special comfort stations," in which some 70,000 Japanese women served Allied soldiers. They did have grounds for concern: within ten days of the Occupation, there were more than 1,300 reported cases of rape in Tokyo's neighboring prefecture of Kanazawa alone. The Tokyo area operated thirty-three state-run brothels, the first of which, located in Omori, was opened on the same day that the Americans landed at Atsugi. The largest, known as the International Palace, was situated in Funabashi, a little east of Tokyo. American customers lined up at one end of the building as they waited to enter; once their time was up, they exited at the other end, where they were politely handed their freshly polished boots. The Paradise in the suburbs of Tachikawa, the Oasis in Ginza, and the Paramount in Shinagawa were other, more centrally located establishments that enjoyed a steady business.

In a reinterpretation of the demands made on the Japanese to sacrifice themselves during the war, the Home Ministry ordered that local associations of prostitutes be established to serve the needs of foreigners. This was packaged as a heroic act of self-sacrifice to protect the purity of the nation. A formal inauguration of "special prostitutes," many of them widows and orphans, was held outside the Imperial Palace. General MacArthur had the RAA facilities closed down in January 1946, but prostitution remained rampant, with many of the brothels remodeling themselves as members of the inventively named "Tea Shop Sanitation

Associations" and "Café Associations."

Japanese women willing to fraternize with US servicemen on an intimate basis were alluded to as *pan pan* girls, and were considered a product of defeat. Many Japanese regarded them with barely concealed contempt, not least for their habit of wearing garish, provocative clothes, smoking, spitting, and bellowing out "Hey, Johnnie!" There was more affection for the name among the young Americans who sought out their company beneath the railway arches of Yurakucho, a district where the Nichigeki Theater, a hall providing cinema screenings, striptease shows, and revues featuring lines of chorus girls, was also located. Other tastes were catered for in Ueno Park, where cross-dressing *dansho* (male prostitutes) established their turf. A sizeable number of foreign homosexuals billeted throughout the city led to the establishment of many gay bars in Tokyo, a phenomenon that had not existed before the war. The writer Mishima Yukio was a frequent visitor to one of the best-known gay cafés, the Brunswick, on the Ginza.

Black markets sprang up like weeds among the rubble, putting down tough roots all over the city. A conservative figure places the number of black-market stalls in Tokyo at the beginning of 1946 at 60,000. They were not universally liked, but were seen as a necessary evil. Many of the goods came from the looting of wartime factories, Japanese army and navy stockpiles, and American warehouses. Some of the items were traded by the *pan pan* girls—goods received as tokens of affection or partial payment from US servicemen. To create the illusion of plenty and to fire up the city's old mercantile spirit, the black markets sold anything they could get hold of, from old socks, turnips, and crockery to pig offal and bloodstained hospital-issued blankets.

Other thriving black markets existed at Tsukiji, the site of the outer marketplace; and Ameyoko, which survives today as a cut-price shopping street with department stores and market stalls, but was once a thriving black market site in a district of flophouses, brothels, and bars. Akihabara, an area now synonymous with quality electronic goods, got its start as a black market. Akihabara Station's rise as a junction between the important Yamanote and Sobu lines coincided with a scarcity of spare radio parts. Stalls were eventually established beneath the tracks of the Sobu Line in 1951, the beginnings of today's shopping behemoth. The station plaza and nearby streets of Shibuya, which had been flattened and carbonized during the air raids, provided ample space for a black market run by Chinese from Taiwan. In July 1946, fearing that the district was being turned into a bolt-hole for Chinese criminal elements, the police moved to close the black market down, setting off violent clashes that resulted in several deaths and injuries. The largest black market of all lined the road from the Isetan department store to Shinjuku Station. The commodities street, lit at night by naked electric bulbs, was christened Hikari Wa Shinjuku, "Bright Shining Shinjuku," but was better known as Ryugu, the "Dragon Palace."

For those who ran the markets, profits could be high. Many right-wing politicians and well-connected gangsters would owe their careers to the markets. Food shortages, however, remained severe. A year after the surrender, a "Give Us Rice" demonstration was held in the city. A larger "Food Mayday" event took place shortly afterward, in which 250,000 Tokyo residents participated. In a city where GIs casually tossed sticks of chewing gum at children smoking discarded cigarette butts, malnutrition persisted, evident in the callow faces, thin blood, and completely white fingernails of the afflicted.

Photographer Hayashi Tadahiko found inspiration in his wanderings around the ruined city. His grainy images capture this hastily built, temporary Tokyo in telling images of ramshackle wooden homes, demobbed soldiers, drinking dens and bars set up on garbage pits, bicycle rickshaws, and striptease joints. In his 1946 photo "A Smoking Street Waif," two half-naked children, unscrubbed but unbowed, are captured as they share a smoke in

Ueno Park, where the statue of Saigo Takamori was being coopted, as it had been during the great 1923 earthquake, as a notice board by people searching for missing relatives.

Tokyo was learning to accommodate its occupying bodies. The screen actress and singer Yamaguchi Yoshiko, better known as Ri Koran, gave a concert to Allied troops at the Hibiya Theater, where, dressed in a slinky silk kimono imprinted with pink cherry blossoms, she performed the "Tokyo Boogie-Woogie" and "I Get a Kick Out of You" to a delirious crowd of GIs. The Teitoza Theater in Shinjuku enjoyed avid patronage from both locals and American servicemen after it hosted the country's first (rather tame) strip show, *The Birth of Venus*.

Cinemas could be found everywhere. Besides conventional film theaters like the old Takarazuka Theater, now renamed the Ernie Pyle, improvised venues were set up in the ruined basements of department stores, under the arches of blackened railway tracks, and in alleys that you had to squeeze along to find. These temporary film houses were necessary, as the Japanese were not allowed into places like the Ernie Pyle. Alternatives existed, however, in venues like the Chikyuza in Shinjuku, where highbrow Russian and European films were soon being screened. Those who attended more local Japanese cinemas in places like Asakusa recall the smell of the audiences, a not-altogether-unpleasant mix of flesh, rice, sweat, and camellia hair oil.

Cinema was already beginning to imitate reality. Visitors to the set of the film *Sounds of Spring* were astounded to find a ruined Tokyo street just like the ones that could be seen a stone's throw from the studio. Real scenes of the destruction visited on the city were rarely shown onscreen during the Occupation. Many of the highly flammable, nitrate-based films documenting the physical aspects of Tokyo were lost in the firebombing of the city. Many others that were not burnt in the raids, but were deemed unsuitable for public consumption by the new authorities, ended up melting in the fires of the US censors. SCAP's list of prohibited subjects included films, books, and plays concerned with militarism; feudal loyalty; anti-foreign sentiment; and revenge themes. Even Mount Fuji was the subject of censorship, being a wartime symbol of nationalism and the backdrop to many propaganda images. Of course, SCAP couldn't remove the offending mountain, but they could delete it from films. When Makino Masahiro explained that he wished to include shots of Mount Fuji in his film *A Fashionable Wanderer*, he was told to excise the offending image as it was a symbol of nationalism. (At least Makino wasn't dragged off to a cell when he commented to the Americans that perhaps they should have bombed the mountain instead of Hiroshima and Nagasaki.)

Restraints on union activities applied even in the arts. A labor demonstration at Toho's Tokyo movie studio in 1948, in contravention of MacArthur's new ban on strikes, ended after US tanks and troops were moved in. In works like Ozu Yasujiro's 1947 *Record of a Tenement Gentleman* and Kurosawa Akira's realist film-noir title *Stray Dog,* censorship limited the footage to the outside of wood and scrap-metal hovels and scorched walls, leaving it to viewers' imaginations to infer what might lie beyond. Hotta Nobuo's documentary film *Time of Darkness* had another effect. A well-known Marxist before the war, one who paid a high price for his beliefs, Hotta had made a documentary that included footage of kamikaze missions, the bombing of Shanghai, and the Nanking Massacre. Its images of the emperor in military uniform, implying a degree of war responsibility, may explain why the film opened in a small art cinema in Shinjuku after larger film distributors refused to deal with it. For his principles, Hotta received several anonymous death threats.

Politics became an issue in films toward the end of the Occupation. Imai Tadashi's 1951 excursion into realism, *And Yet We Live*, was shot with a hidden camera and the participation of the left-wing drama troupe Zenshin-za. Filmed on the streets around Ueno Station, the content, focusing on the exploitation of workers, was deemed likely to incite unrest; this, of course, was precisely the director's intention. In the middle of making *Children of the Beehive*, director Yamamoto Satsuo was ordered not to include members of the Occupation in the frame. English signs, areas eviscerated by bombs, and even GI jeeps were to be removed. As historian John Dower remarked, "The 'occupied' screen did not merely offer a new, imagined world. It also made things disappear."

All new screenplays and book titles were carefully scanned by the Civil Information and Education Section, a special office tasked with the ironic job of weeding out any work expressing anti-democratic, sentiments along with any ideas demonstrating opposition to SCAP orders. Over half of the 500 films examined were destroyed in the 1946 bonfires, an irretrievable loss. Any references to the American air raids on Tokyo and other cities were prohibited. Books and films on the atomic bombings of Hiroshima and Nagasaki were similarly banned.

In the same way that precious Buddhist works of art had been willfully destroyed in the Meiji era, the zeal for renewal could at times result in the evisceration of culture. Film companies, induced to think of their past masterpieces as feudal, consigned them to the incinerator. The big hit song of 1951 was "Tears of Nagasaki," signaling a change of mood, a graduated erosion of deference toward the occupiers.

In Japan's counterpart to the Nuremberg trials, the International Military Tribune for the Far East (better known as the Tokyo trial), the dice were heavily loaded, with eleven judges from each of the occupied nations hearing evidence against twenty-eight prominent Japanese who had been in power from 1928 to 1945. Unlike at Nuremberg, there were no innocent verdicts, though two defendants died and one—the fanatic ideologue Okawa Shumei—was declared insane. The verdicts—seven death sentences, sixteen life incarcerations, two shorter sentences—were predictable enough, given the court's flawed procedures.

One of the judges, a Filipino, was a survivor of the Bataan Death March. The trial was notable for its omissions: the emperor was not indicted or even required to testify; details of the murder of Chinese soldiers and civilians as a result of vivisections and exposure to bacteria like plague and cholera at a Japanese chemical and biological warfare detachment based in Pingfan, close to Harbin, were not elaborated on. An immunity deal had already been sealed between the US, eager to acquire the knowledge gained from the experiments, and the Japanese scientists and doctors who had worked for the so-called Unit 731. These men returned to normal society, several of the top members going on to successful careers in science and medicine, some even opening their own hospitals. War crimes and atrocities conducted by the Allies, such as the atomic bombings, the carpet-bombing of civilian areas of Tokyo, and the Soviet Union's attack on Japan in the final days of the war and its treatment of Japanese soldiers, were not addressed.

The US and Britain, in preparing the military tribunals in Germany and Japan, had gone to some lengths to pre-exonerate themselves from accusations of war crimes. These included two new categories: "crimes against humanity" and "crimes against peace." It was, as wartime prime minister Tojo Hideki memorably put it, a case of "victor's justice." Predictably, Tojo, with his tortoiseshell glasses and skull as smooth as an ostrich egg, fiercely unrepentant in his nationalism and displaying visible contempt for the proceedings, was the centerpiece of the trial. Black-market prices were paid to obtain entrance to the court during his cross-examinations. A stickler for detail, Tojo took full responsibility for his actions during the war, but made one unrehearsed slip that brought the entire proceedings to a halt. "None of us," he declared, "would have dared act against the emperor's will." Pressure was put on him to rescind the statement, and Tojo appeared a week later, affirming that the emperor had always issued for peace. After a spartan meal of cold rice and sake, Tojo was hanged in Sugamo prison in December 1948. All the trial convicts who survived were paroled after the Occupation and unconditionally released in 1958.

Political prisoners were among the first to be liberated when the Occupation began. Left-wing writers who had either been imprisoned or driven into hiding returned to Tokyo, resuming their work with a new passion. With the resurgence in print of some of Japan's literary giants, among them Tanizaki Junichiro, Osaragi Jiro, and Shiga Naoya, new magazines were published. In the year 1946 alone, sixty new titles appeared on the shelves. The renaissance of publishing and the arts reflected a renewed craving for culture in a city that was physically expanding. Tokyo's thirty-five war-decimated wards were reorganized into a more manageable twenty-two in March, 1947. They would later be re-consolidated to twenty-three. The Local Autonomy Act that made this possible had the effect of turning the city into a self-governing entity similar to those enjoyed by prefectural governments. By 1950, the population, reduced to 3,480,000 by the end of the war, had recovered to 6,270,000.

Compared with their counterparts in Europe after the war, collaborators from Japan's literary and art circles appear to have gotten off lightly. For the most part, artists who had supported the war cause simply blended back into civilian life once daily routines resumed. Many of them continued to publish or have their work displayed. Even Hayashi Fumiko, a respected novelist who had turned her skills towards war reportage and become an embedded journalist for the Imperial Army, reporting from Nanking, where the military had committed a notorious massacre, was forgiven her lapses by a public that was hardly blameless, having itself passionately supported the war in its early stages.

On the grounds that the emperor supported the Occupation and that his removal would create social upheaval, civil disobedience or worse, Hirohito, whose failings as a sovereign during the war were arguably crimes of omission rather than execution, was spared. "Thus," as Donald Richie put it, "the single most feudal object of all, the imperial system, remained unpurged." The question of the emperor's culpability will always be a vexing one. As both divine paterfamilias and supreme commander of the imperial armed forces, the war was fought in his name and carried—however reluctantly in the beginning—his official endorsement and agreement for war mobilization. In the months of indecision near the end of the war, when Hirohito was pressing for "another dazzling military gain" for Japan so that it could negotiate a peace deal on more favorable terms for the nation, countless lives were lost.

The obfuscation of historical reality in Japan is partly attributable to the documentation of imperial affairs by the government and the Imperial Household Agency, which mirrors the ancient Chinese approach to historiography. The function of history in imperial China was not the objective interpretation of facts, but the legitimization of the current dynasty. Accordingly, Chinese history was rewritten to empower each new dynasty. Similarly, the official view of imperial history in Japan, despite coming under scrutiny from more objective quarters, exists not to illuminate truth but to exonerate the imperial institution. Because the emperor acted behind the scenes during the war years, his advisers were able to insist that his function was merely to rubber-stamp decisions made by others. Despite the emperor's having sanctioned the invasion of China in 1937, being cognizant of the usage of chemical weapons in China, and enthusing over the attack on Pearl Harbor, history—with the endorsement of the Allied military occupation personnel headed by General Mac-Arthur—succeeded in perpetrating the image of a benign and blameless figurehead. The emperor, aloof and reclusive when required, energetic when it was expedient to be so, was rather good at projecting contrasting images of his role and interactions with the imperial court, politicians, and generals.

The emperor's personal visit to pay his respects to MacArthur on September 27, 1945, was significant not only for its attempt to establish a rapport between the two men and to determine the course of the occupation, but for the photograph that was taken of the meeting and featured on the front pages of every major newspaper in the country. The general, resting his hands on his hips and towering above the diminutive figure of the emperor, appears relaxed. He is not wearing a tie. Hirohito, clothed in morning dress belonging to a different age, stands next to the general in a rigid pose, as if he is reviewing a military parade of his ghost troops. For the Japanese viewer, the picture stood for nothing less than the defeat of Japan by an enemy that was stronger, technically and militarily more powerful, and materially richer.

The two men, who stood in front of the lens like the very embodiments of Defeat and Victory portrayed in a Greek play, had nonetheless found common ground and mutual respect. The effort on the Occupation forces' part—and by subsequent Japanese governments and the Imperial Household Agency—to transform the image of the much-photographed warrior on a white steed into a blameless postwar symbol of peace would not be complete, perhaps, until 1975, when the emperor was snapped in the company of Mickey Mouse and other cuddly friends while on a visit to Disneyland in Los Angeles.

War crimes were one thing; daily felonies—rampant at this time—were another. In such desperate times, you could have your throat cut for a bag of sugar bought on the black market. House thefts were common, and parks were too dangerous for women to enter at night. Prostitution remained legal, highly profitable for those involved in the business, and ubiquitous. Yakuza involvement in everything from petty crime to politics and the construction industry increased to a record high. Part of the *après-guerre* scene was the use of hard liquor and drugs. *Hiropon* (methamphetamine) was tantamount to a street commodity. The stimulant was used by many laborers hired as part of the city's postwar reconstruction program.

An altogether different crime occurred on the afternoon of January 26, 1948, at the Teikoku Bank in Shinamachi, near Ikebukuro. A man claiming to be one Dr. Yamaguchi Jiro, Ministry of Health and Welfare inspector, presented himself at the branch bank and demanded to see the manager. Explaining that there had been an outbreak of dysentery from an infected neighborhood well, he ordered members of the staff to take two doses of a medication he provided from a case of labeled bottles. Within minutes, the man exited the bank, having removed only a relatively small amount of money, leaving behind a large amount of untouched cash and sixteen bodies, twelve of whom would perish, writhing in their death throes after drinking what was apparently a cyanide solution. A suspect—an artist with no ostensible alibi but with a history of memory loss, psychosis, and a disorder known as amnestic-confabulatory syndrome—was eventually arrested; after daily interrogation over a two-month period, the man confessed to the crime. Serious misgivings about the actual identity of the person responsible for one of Tokyo's most sinister crimes remain, however, to this day.

In the early summer of the same year, the public was shocked to hear of the double suicide of writer Dazai Osamu and his lover when their bodies were found washed up in the rain-swollen Tamagawa Canal in western Tokyo. A highly gifted wastrel who had frittered away his family's allowance on women, drink, and a serious drug habit, Dazai had composed masterworks like *Ningen Shikkaku* (No Longer Human) and *Shayo* (The Setting Sun) that were avidly read by young people who shared his grim vision of the human condition.

Dazai's novels, like everyone else's, had been put through the blender of censorship. Though considerably less severe than wartime Japanese censorship, the Occupation version was, arguably, more insidious in the sense that it was difficult to identify. During the war, newspapers, journals, and other published materials had been crudely defaced by crosses, blank spaces, and inserted circles indicating where the offending passages were. This practice was not continued under the Occupation, making it near impossible to know exactly what had been censored. Helen Mear's 1948 book *Mirror for Americans: Japan*—a work highly critical of the premises upon which the Occupation was based—did not go down well with the authorities. MacArthur personally stepped in to make sure that the book was not translated into Japanese. In a curious example of double standards, at the same time SCAP was promoting free speech, it was also prohibiting any discussion or criticism of its policies. MacArthur's towering self-esteem; the speeches, grandstanding, and decrees that issued from his headquarters—these were no less imperious or absolute than Hirohito's had been during the war. When SCAP officials heard of a Tokyo vaudeville actor performing a song with the line, "Everyone is blabbering about democracy, but how can we have democracy when there are two emperors?" the song was immediately banned, the hapless singer given a dressing-down.

When China fell to the communists, the Occupation authorities, having formally encouraged the formation of labor unions and liberal socialism, now moved to undermine both. Occupation officials moved to expel communist sympathizers from educational institutes and the civil service, then mounted a purge on the media. In retrospect, Occupation censorship seems fussy and overweening, but even at its most draconian, it could not compare to the stultifying controls exercised during the war years.

Small liberties were emerging. New weekly magazines were launched in 1952. In August of that year, *Asahi Graph* released full-page spreads of photographs showing A-bomb victims for the first time. The response was massive; 700,000 copies of the issue sold. In this pre-TV age, the streets were still lively, interactive spaces. *Kamishibai* (picture-story shows) were at the height of their popularity in 1949, with some 50,000 storytellers performing narratives with illustrated cards to audiences of young children as a way to sell candy and crackers. During the war the government had used *kamishibai* for propaganda purposes. Now, during the Occupation, the Americans were doing the same, promoting stories centered on Western values.

Things were looking up for children. In response to their requests, Indian Prime Minister Jawaharlal Nehru presented an elephant to the children of Japan in September 1949. Although it stepped off the ship at midnight, the fifteen-year-old giant, named after the Nehru's daughter Indira, was welcomed by a massive crowd of children, who thronged its route all the way from Shibaura Port to Ueno Zoo. The young spectators were awed into silence by the sheer size of the lumbering pachyderm. Some of the adults lining the streets to the zoo may have reflected on the sight of an animal that embodied the magnificence of India, a country whose northern borders Japanese troops had invaded only a few short years before, walking through the nocturnal streets of the occupied city.

Atop the National Olympic Stadium, the cauldron for the flame that illuminated the 1964 summer games. Tokyo is the first Asian city to host the Olympic Games twice. (Photo by Dddeco, printed under the Creative Commons Attribution-Share Alike 3.0 Unported License)

CHAPTER 7

The Independent City

A hazardous environment – The Tokyo Olympics – Protests –
A bubble economy – Another new city

In the autumn of 1954, Tokyo citizens recoiled in horror at the sight of a large reptilian creature emerging from the waters of Tokyo Bay. During its rampage through the capital, much of the city was destroyed, including the National Diet Building.

The darkly prophetic screenplay of the first *Godzilla* film appearing in cinemas that year reflected not just the anxieties of the immediate postwar years, but an incident that had occurred just eight months before the release of the blockbuster. On March 1 of that year, the crew of the fishing boat *Daigo Fukuryu Maru* was exposed to radiation following a hydrogen bomb test conducted by the US Army in the Pacific region of Bikini Atoll in the Marshall Islands. On returning to Tokyo, the ship's chief radio operator died, and the event sparked outrage and passionate antinuclear demonstrations. Godzilla, a creature reawakened from a centuries-long slumber in the aftermath of a nuclear test, embodied an almost visceral fear of such monstrous experimentation.

Tokyo's rate of reconstruction in the face of natural calamities, self-destructive human errors, and the mutation that was Godzilla was astonishing. The English writer Angus Wilson, visiting the city in 1957, noted, "The new Tokyo promises to be impressive rather than beautiful…at the back of my mind was always the feeling that Tokyo, city of natural disasters, was the model of the future cities of the world in an atomic age—a mixture of improvised shoddiness and eternal rebuilding."

Another Englishman, the poet James Kirkup, experiencing the city two years on, would write, "The first impression one receives is not so much of a city as of some huge, shapeless industrial suburb, extremely ugly and noisy." He did append the comment, though, that "despite the drabness and grimness of Tokyo, the vivacious, vital, vibrant and volatile Japanese people themselves transform their city into the liveliest and most fantastic place in the modern world."

The perilous state of the Japanese economy in the early 1950s received an unexpected boost with the commencement of hostilities on the Korean Peninsula in June, 1950. It cannot have failed to strike some Japanese as ironic that their country, which only a few years earlier had found itself in a death struggle with the United States, was now provisioning its former enemy with the means to fight another war in Asia. Japan was no longer the enemy of the West but an important strategic partner, an ally experiencing the stirrings of an economic boom. The special procurement contracts that Japan was awarded at the start of the war galvanized its economy: in 1947, the number of commercial offices in the city in 1947 stood at 281,000. By 1954 it had grown to 359,000.

A similar proliferation was taking place among the numerous religious sects based in Tokyo during the postwar period, a phenomenon known as the "rush hour of the gods." These groups offered any number of means for escapist bliss, though some of the staggering claims they made elicited more mirth than devotion. "The moment I open my mouth," the female founder of the Dancing Religion sect claimed, "the Divine Radio commences, and you can listen to revelations straight from God." Similarly— politics being the next-best thing to faith—Tokyo witnessed a great surge in ideologies at this time. By the 1960s the world had become increasingly polarized along ideologically opposing lines, and Japan was no exception. Disaffected Tokyo youth found issues to protest in the 1952 Anti-Subversion Law and ANPO, the US–Japan Security Treaty. Under the influence of union leaders, members of the Communist Party, and left-leaning intellectuals, a huge gathering of workers and students staged a protest against the treaty on May Day, 1952. Two people were killed and countless numbers injured and trampled after the crowd confronted riot police armed with tear gas, guns, and batons.

Political changes in Japan and the advent of the Cold War saw a return to power of conservative leaders purged after the war. Kishi Nobusuke had been a signatory of the declaration of war against the United States in 1941, and was subsequently imprisoned as a war-crimes suspect tasked with organizing industrial projects in Manchuria; he had had served as Minister of Munitions in the Tojo cabinet. The possibility that a public figure with such a past could be elected to the position of prime minister in 1957 would have been inconceivable just a few years earlier. The existence of a more bellicose Russia, China, and North Korea changed everything, however. A staunch anticommunist who favored a strong military alliance with the United States, Kishi was considered Washington's point man in Tokyo. Millions of dollars were funneled to him and other leaders of the Liberal Democratic Party by the CIA.

Demonstrators tried to prevent Kishi's plane from taking off from Haneda Airport, but a fresh security treaty was signed in Washington on January 19, 1960. When the prime minister insisted that the Diet pass the vote on the treaty without adding amendments, almost 600,000 people took to the streets of the capital. More protests erupted after news surfaced that Kishi and his party had rammed the extension of the treaty through the Lower House. Socialist Party MPs who had staged a sit-in protest were ejected by police with the aid of right-wing "public secretaries."

As demonstrators organized by Zengakuren, the nationwide union of students and radical left-wing groups gathered, Kishi sent a top-ranking aide to meet in secret with Tokyo gangland bosses, who swiftly recruited some 20,000 yakuza and more than 10,000 extreme rightists to attack the demonstrators. Kishi provided lavish funds to provision them with helicopters, trucks, a liaison base, food, and other amenities. Yakuza bosses and their stooges were in the Diet Building on the night of the special Diet session, helping to suppress protest by blocking the doors to opponents of the ratification who were gathering outside. Some student rioters expressed their rage by urinating on the entrance stairways to the National Diet building.

Populist resentment swelled once again on June 10, when US Ambassador Douglas MacArthur II and a White House press secretary arrived to prepare the way for President Eisenhower's visit the following week. The group was met by thousands of protesters at the airport, where their car was attacked and they were forced to make a swift exit in a US Marine helicopter. On June 15, 1960, 100,000 demonstrators gathered in Hibiya Park marching on to the Diet Building to protest against the Revised Security Treaty. Seven thousand demonstrators led by the All-Japan Federation of Students broke through the south gate of the building and clashed with riot police, who responded with tear gas. A young Tokyo student named Kanba Michiko was killed in the press, achieving a kind of martyrdom when she was dubbed the "Jeanne d'Arc of the student movement." Eisenhower's trip was cancelled. Kishi resigned on June 23, followed by his entire cabinet the next month.

Japan's complicity in the Vietnam War was seemingly confirmed by its lucrative—though non-combative—collusion in it through the procurement business, and the government's tolerance of the ongoing US military occupation of Okinawa, where American bomber planes took off with massive payloads, and marines rehearsed the conflict in Indochina in the island's northern jungles. This supplied further fuel to the incendiary atmosphere of a city now metabolizing into a political battlefield.

An activist group called Beiheren, the Citizen's League for Peace in Vietnam, helped US deserters go underground in Tokyo and attempted to disrupt stockholders' meetings at the Mitsubishi Corporation, which was making huge profits from the war. The streets of Shinjuku were the ideal platform for the activities of both peaceniks with acoustic guitars and activists advocating firebombs and revolution. On October 21, 1968, which was International Anti-War Day, some 2,000 young people took control of Shinjuku Station in an incident that became known as the Shinjuku Riot. Trains were blocked and carriages set on fire in protest at Japan National Railways' complicity in the Vietnam War by allowing freight and fuel to be carried to US military bases. During the night of the troubles, around 450 people were arrested. The following year, 7,000 self-styled "folk guerrillas" gathered in the station's subterranean tunnels and walkways to sing antiwar songs. This time the police used tear gas before making arrests.

Strikes had already broken out at Tokyo's prestigious Waseda University in 1966; the students, supported by opposition groups and many sympathetic members of the public, stayed away for 155 days. In 1968, strikes among medical students at Tokyo University, the nation's foremost seat of learning, spread to other faculties there and almost 200 other universities nationwide. By October, Tokyo University campuses at Hongo and Komaba were at a virtual standstill. Entrance exams scheduled for the following year were cancelled.

Initially, Tokyo University student concerns were centered on the democratization of their own campus: fairly modest aspirations to reform the outdated institution, improve the poor content of lectures, and align outmoded bureaucratic practices with the contemporary academic world. Popular resistance to the Vietnam War and the US–Japan Security Treaty added to the discontent, leading to the seizure of the Yasuda Auditorium, a nine-story clock tower located on the campus. The Tokyo Metropolitan Police Department reacted swiftly, mobilizing 8,500 officers in riot gear to remove the students from the building. The police used 10,000 tear gas grenades and sprayed gas from helicopters; water cannons and powerful fire engines were used to smash barricaded windows and doors. Students counterattacked by dropping broken flagstones and assorted items of furniture from the roof of the tower. Worn down and cornered, the police retaliated by beating and kicking students into submission. Some 270 of the 400 students arrested on the spot were injured, many seriously. One student was blinded. The police took a battering as well, with 710 wounded in the battle.

In May 1969, some of the city's most disputatious students, members of the radical Zenkyoto (United Front), met the brilliant writer Mishima Yukio, a staunch supporter of the imperial system, for a debate at the Komaba campus of Tokyo University. Even though he knew students had taken hostages before and that the atmosphere could turn hostile, Mishima refused the police protection he was offered. He did, however, wind a cotton *haramaki* around his stomach as protection against a possible knife thrust. Ironically enough, a year later it would be Mishima himself wielding such a blade.

Early in the morning of November 25, 1970, Mishima sealed a package to his publisher containing the last installment of his novel *The Decay of the Angel*, the final volume of his *Sea of Fertility* tetralogy. At 11 a.m., accompanied by four cadets from his private paramilitary group known as the Tatenokai, or Shield Society, he arrived at the Ichigaya headquarters of the Eastern Army and proceeded to the office of General Mashita Kanetoshi. After blocking the doors and tying the general to a chair, Mishima appeared on the balcony of the office and delivered a speech to a crowd of soldiers and reporters. The din from the jeering audience, helicopters overhead, and policemen revving their motorbikes drowned out most of Mishima's rant, in which he read a manifesto calling for the restoration of the imperial system and a return to wartime Japanese values. After crying out "Long live His Majesty the Emperor" three times, Mishima withdrew to the office, knelt on its carpet and proceeded to commit seppuku, ritual disembowelment. When the chosen cadet failed to complete the *coup de grâce* after three deplorably clumsy attempts, another of the group took up the sword and completed the beheading. If Mishima had hoped to stir nationalist indignation and revolt among the armed forces, or to trigger an imperial restoration by putting the steel and muscle back in Japan, his speech was a signal failure. In a press photo taken of Mishima making his appeal from the balcony of General Mashita's office, the camera angle inadvertently renders the figure in a diminished, attenuated form, a man shrunk by his own fury.

Amid the tainted political climate, Tokyoites breathed their own air with growing concern. The civic pride instilled in Tokyo residents upon the 1959 announcement that the city had won its bid to host the Olympic Games was moderated by the appalling environmental conditions prevalent in the city. Tens of thousands of people filed claims each year to the Tokyo Metropolitan Government for compensation for smog-related ailments. Emissions from smoke stacks, steel mills, power plants, and dump fires forced many residents to wear face masks or buy oxygen from vending machines.

Soot particles in the air were on the decrease, but more worrying was the spike in sulfur dioxide and carbon monoxide levels, which were at an all-time high with the approaching Olympics. The pallid curtain of smog grew denser with the increase in car emissions. First-aid stations were set up to assist people overcome by the toxic air, and pavement cafés were fronted by plastic drapes to deter the dust, smoke, and smell of setting cement that filled the odiferous city. "Air pollution in Tokyo," observed Kawanami Yoshiaki, a member of the Public Nuisance Department, "could soon become as serious as the situation in London."

In the highly industrial city of the 1960s and 1970s, it was easy to identify the source of the noxious air: it poured from the chimneys of coal-burning steelworks, furnaces, canneries, foundries, glass-making factories, and petrochemical plants. Coal-fired taxis, a fixture of the immediate postwar years, had long since vanished, but the smoke from kerosene-, wood-, or charcoal-and-rice-husk-fueled kitchen stoves; from refuse incinerators and demolition areas where old lumber from wooden framed buildings, rafters, and lintels were still burnt on site; and from the rusting oil drums used by laborers intensified the pollution. Nighttime hawkers of corn on the cob, roast chestnuts, and sweet potatoes added more savory smells to the smoky city.

The election, on April 15, 1967, of Minobe Ryokichi as Tokyo governor—an office he held for three terms until 1979—was quite literally, a breath of fresh air. His slogan "Let's Bring Back Blue Skies to Tokyo," was a riposte to the government's preference for fast-tracking economic development, speculative real-estate investment, and unbridled corporate expansion at the expense of welfare reform and environmental concerns. Freezing funding for some of the more superfluous highway construction in the city and introducing traffic-free pedestrian malls, his most significant reform was the enactment of the Tokyo Metropolitan Pollution Ordinance, which put pressure on heavy industry to relocate outside city limits. Although other problems remained, smog would be almost entirely eliminated within the next decade.

One of the major projects of the postwar period was a 333-meter-high transmission structure known as the Tokyo Tower. Its main function was to send waves that would transmit television images. Following the suspension of the Korean War in 1953, there was a surplus of US arms in Japan. As industrial-quality metals were in short supply, the contractors for Tokyo Tower obtained 300 retired US tanks and recycled them into steel frames, which were used to construct the upper section of the tower. Several people died during the difficult construction process.

Some people held that the accidents were the result of a curse: one of the tower's iron legs stood in the former graveyard of the Tokugawa shoguns, located in the old compound of Zojo-ji temple. The opening ceremony took place on Christmas Eve, 1958. The patriotic goal of the construction was to show a city emerging from the devastation of war and taking its place alongside the international community, although the structure, which was unabashedly modeled on the Eiffel Tower, attracted little attention overseas. A classic example of duplitecture, the tower was viewed by foreigners as a poor knockoff at best, representing all that was vulgar and ill-conceived in modern Japan. To the Japanese, however, it symbolized progress.

There was soon to be an even bigger project than Tokyo Tower, one with the avowed aim of gaining Japan readmission into the international community. It was an event that would chase away the subtle shadows, the nuanced shades and grains of an older city savored by writers such as Nagai Kafu, and replace them with the remorseless brilliance of a blindingly bright new capital. More than two-thirds of the budget for the "Trillion-Yen Olympics," as the undertaking was known, was earmarked for infrastructure spending. The subsequent transformation in the appearance of the city included the construction of the Tokaido Shinkansen train connecting the capital with Osaka, 100 kilometers of new superhighways, and a monorail linking downtown Tokyo with Haneda International Airport. After the war, the old drill grounds at Yoyogi in Shibuya ward had been requisitioned as land to house American military personnel and their dependents. Known as "Washington Heights," the site was returned to the Japanese to build an Olympic Village. Delays were inevitable as the date for the Games loomed. Construction of an elevated coastal highway to Haneda Airport was held up because fishermen owning land along the route were demanding exorbitant amounts of money to sell. In other parts of the city, plots of land earmarked by the government for development had already been bought up by speculators, who were holding out for higher prices.

Another headache for the Olympic planners was a water shortage. Reservoirs should have filled up in the months preceding the event, but the rains had failed to materialize. In a frenzy of activity, artesian wells were dug, canals connected to new river sources, dry ice deposited on clouds by Japan Self-Defense Force planes, and water rationing introduced in an effort to alleviate the problem. Just outside the city at the Ogochi reservoir, a Shinto priest wearing a red lion mask conducted a ritual rain dance. The public was told not to expect instant results. As the holy man put it, "It might take as long as two days for the prayers to get through to the dragon god."

Ichikawa Kon's 1965 documentary masterpiece *Tokyo Olympiad* was a massive undertaking, involving a staff of almost six hundred. The Olympic Organizing Board, who wanted a film that would glorify the Games and highlight Japanese athletes, got instead a film that showed them in a touchingly human manner, coming in third rather than first, collapsed in exhaustion, cramped and agonized; the final scene showed an empty stadium with a single figure walking across the ground carrying a ladder. It would be decades before the uncut version of the film was shown. The documentary highlighted some of the impressive Olympic buildings, including Tange Kenzo's magisterial National Gymnasium complex, a design that would go on to win him the Pritzker Prize for architecture. The Olympics, and the pharaonic scale of re-planning they required, propelled Tokyo into the niche of one of the wealthiest cities in the world.

New subway lines were created, as well as access roads to the city and the Olympic pavilions. The number of construction sites for road building and street improvement alone during those short years rose to 10,000. The annoyance from nocturnal roadwork crews operating diesel compressors and powerful lights, forced residents to hang black curtains over their windows and resort to earplugs to block out the racket.

The surging vitality, presaging the next three decades of exhilarating economic growth, eclipsed any concerns about preserving traces of the old city. In an example of expediency trumpeting heritage, the new Shuto Express's Number 4 Loop Line was installed above the Nihonbashi Bridge. The majestic structure, effectively diminished by the pragmatic vulgarities of city planners, was consigned to chilly shadows and visual obscurity. To obviate the cost and delays involved in purchasing land, many overhead expressways were built above canals and rivers. Other waterways were filled in with building debris and rubble. Where channels remained, water stagnated and fish died in an unholy cocktail of raw sewage and biochemical sludge, turning once-enchanting waterways into putrid cesspools.

Regulations limiting building heights in the Marunouchi district to eight floors out of respect for the Imperial Palace—which, it was held, should never be cast in shadow—were being tested as early as the 1950s. By the time of the Olympics, the custom of keeping a protective Buddha statue under the roof of buildings was no longer observed. Other cleanup efforts dated from the days before the Olympics. Prior to the event, the government let it be known Westerners did not appreciate the sight of public urination, and signs were put up in the subways to that effect. Whether by coercion or consent, the numerous streetwalkers in the city's entertainment districts and the population of homeless people and beggars in Ueno Park vanished from sight. Another casualty of the city's fierce determination to make itself presentable to the world were some 200,000 stray or abandoned cats and dogs, all rounded up and exterminated by carbon dioxide.

Inevitably, the developments were uneven. The rapidly growing prosperity of the 1960s and the city's embrace of an Americanized culture could not transcend its persistent poverty. In an article on the Olympics written for *Life* magazine, Arthur Koestler observed that Tokyo was the "first city in the world with a monorail system linking airport to urban center, but it has no citywide sewage system." Fewer than a quarter of the city's twenty-three wards, in fact, had anything like a modern sewage system. Human waste was sucked up from beneath buildings by vacuum trucks that made their way around the city, impregnating the air with their stench. Kitchen and bathwater effluents poured into open roadside gutters, where inebriated males would often stop to urinate.

The Olympic Games had a spiritual side, as well. Shinto priests performed purification ceremonies above the newly laid foundations of sports pavilions, and conducted religious rites on the day the kitchens were opened in the Olympic Village. Benign forces may even have had a hand in the final preparation for the Games. On October 8, just two days before the opening ceremony, and with almost all of the infrastructure programs completed in readiness for the big event, a typhoon swept through the streets of Tokyo, cleansing the city of its litter, dust, and air pollution.

Despite the losses and disfigurations, the Games were hailed as a resounding success. At the opening ceremony, as the Olympic flame was being lit by a young man born in Hiroshima on the day the atomic bomb was dropped; Japanese Self-Defense Forces fighter jets scrambled over Tokyo, incising five Olympic rings in the sky. Japanese contestants managed to win a stunning sixteen gold medals, second only to the United States and the Soviet Union. As a sporting event and window on the new Japan, it was a truly Olympian event, marking Japan's acceptance once more into the international community. Tokyo, no longer a third-rate capital, was now a city of light, a gleaming international metropolis.

During the construction boom that characterized the postwar period, rules were notoriously relaxed, building practices shoddy. During that time, the Japanese construction state, a close alliance between high ranking politicians, bureaucrats, and some of the world's most aggressive real estate and property management companies, would transform the city into the center of a massive land-development economy that would see Tokyo sprawl outward into an expanding belt of ill-defined suburbs and *terrains vagues*. Many people had to endure cramped, Soviet-style public housing, some of the dreariest urban environments ever dreamt up in the developed world. Many of these *danchi* were built in haste to accommodate the growing number of people gravitating to the city from the countryside. Part of the problem was the sheer number of people pouring into the city in search of work. Between 1955 and 1965, the population of greater Tokyo grew from 13.2 million to 18.8 million residents. Little wonder housing problems were chronic. Public housing projects run by local municipalities provided tiny, two-bedroom apartments. Separate dining areas and flush toilets, however, set them apart from pre-war housing conditions, and there were few complaints about the indignities of cramped space. Many younger office workers, though, had to settle for poor-quality wooden rental apartments known as *moku-chin apaato*.

The concept of zoning certainly existed, but was only haphazardly implemented. The Metabolist movement in architecture, presided over by Tange Kenzo and younger designers like Isozaki Arata and Kurokawa Kisho, was fueled by the perception of cities as constantly changing organisms with relatively slow rates of change for infrastructure, but rapid replacement of individual buildings. Tange's 1960 *A Plan for Tokyo* project was based on the conviction that a "radical centripetal city like Tokyo would inevitably reach a state of confusion and paralysis as the population grew." Tange and his team advocated a civic axis, a "linear structure capable of growth like a vertebrate animal" for a city that had almost doubled its population between 1950 and 1970. The plan called for a three-level construction of offices, residences, commercial enterprises, and transportation systems that would stretch into Tokyo Bay. Similarly, Isozaki Arata's *City in the Air: Shinjuku Project*, an ambitious design to create groves of interlinking skyscrapers located at key city nodes, was an idea ahead of its time.

The physical city may have looked improvised and uncoordinated, but culture was flourishing again. In the sixties, ideas flowed like hot lava. Playwrights and directors sought out modern subjects rooted in Japanese styles of performance. These included the experimental works of playwrights such as Terayama Shuji, Kara Juro and Suzuki Tadashi. The venues were stridently *avant-garde*; Terayama staged his performances on barges, and in warehouses, lofts, and in the street. One production by the Existential Theater was staged inside a bright yellow tent, which the company pitched wherever they could find space. Venues included riverbanks, car parks, derelict cemeteries, aerodromes, abandoned railway yards, and beside the sacred lotus pond in Ueno Park.

The use of Shinjuku as a psycho-scape for political activism, film showings, and exhibitions of radical art marked a moment when the city was in synchrony with international culture and activism. Rapid urban growth and vertiginous transformations in the media and technology created fertile ground for new forms of inter-media arts. Many underground theaters emerged in the 1960s, among them Tenjo Sajiki and Sasori-za. Takamatsu Jiro and several of his co-conspirators in art staged a "guerrilla performance" event on a Yamanote Line train in October, 1962.

Some of the swaggering conceit and nationalism of the early war years reemerged during the bubble economy years. This gilded age, dating from 1985, was characterized by opulence, waste, corruption, and strong notions of Japanese exceptionalism. An embarrassment of riches led to claims of cultural hegemony and superiority. The city was gripped by the triumphalism that accompanies rapidly amassed affluence and by the realization, in a nation that had been defeated in the war, that the best form of revenge is success. One Japanese businessman became an object of world media attention after he famously quipped that in the new world order, America would become Japan's granary, Australia its mine, and Europe its boutique. Part of the bubble-era braggadocio was the conviction that Japan was immune to the kind of economic viruses that periodically beset the outer world.

There were plenty of after-hours districts, like Roppongi and Shinbashi, serving the same ends, but as an expense-account entertainment district, the Ginza was the undisputed showcase for the display of wealth and its corresponding presumption of infallible cycles of ever-increasing profit. Frequent eyewitness accounts of a man in a business suit doing the rounds of hostess bars with a suitcase stuffed with bank notes may have been representative of the more eccentric habits of Japan's financial barons, but there were myriad other examples of extravagance. Young women dressed in sumptuous silk kimonos and European couture passed nightly through the doors of hostess clubs and bars with names like Platinum, the Monaco, and Club Royale. One establishment boasted mink-upholstered toilet covers; another served single-malt whiskies poured over chunks of ice cut from Alaskan glaciers. Customers were encouraged to listen attentively to the crack and hiss as oxygen was released from the ten-thousand-year-old ice. At Ginza restaurants you could be served desserts covered with flakes of real gold.

With so much money being invested in land, real-estate values went ballistic. Banks lent money to companies and individuals, who bought real estate, thereby increasing the paper value of land assets, which were used as collateral to obtain extended loans that fueled speculation on the stock market and the purchase of more land. The banks continued to grant loans based on overvalued land proffered as collateral. At the height of this asset-driven era, the land value of the Imperial Palace was said to be higher than the real-estate holdings of the entire state of California. With little awareness of how their country was viewed from outside, many Japanese people were shocked to hear of a *Newsweek* poll in which 52 percent of those questioned rated the Japanese economy a "greater threat" to the US than the military power of the Soviet Union.

The enthrallment was temporary. As with all great booms, the momentum eventually ceased. On the last day of 1989, the Bank of Japan stepped in, raising interest rates, forcing land values to conform to the laws of gravity. The American Occupation and the subsequent decades of growth had helped to promote the myth that history could be halted, willfully divided into neat dichotomies of radical discontinuity: prewar and postwar, a divine emperor, a human monarch; an imperium, a democracy; war, peace; darkness and light; poverty and prosperity. History, on the contrary, is a continuum. Tokyo did not enter the next decade a pauper, but its fingers had been severely scorched after the collapse of the bubble economy. Nothing would be quite the same again.

At 6:33 a.m. on January 7, 1989, Emperor Showa, after a sixty-two-year reign, passed away in Fukiage Palace. The man who had personified Japan's conquest of its Asian neighbors and its surrender to the Allied powers had also overseen the extraordinary postwar economic recovery. On February 24, an estimated 200,000 people lined the cold, rain-wet streets of Tokyo to observe the emperor's funeral cortege, accompanied by gongs, drums, and bamboo flutes, as it made its way to the Shinjuku Imperial Gardens, where a Shinto ceremony was held. Representatives from 164 countries attended the service. The Shinto rituals were boycotted by socialist and communist leaders.

While this orchestrated reverence was being conducted under the scrutiny of a massive security force, some 100,000 people in the city attended rallies denouncing the Showa emperor as a war criminal. When an explosion shook the main building of Togo Shrine in Shibuya ward, shattering its main door, collapsing a section of the ceiling, and starting a fire that scorched the pillars of an exterior passage, anti-establishment radicals opposed to the imperial system were held responsible. Several other small explosions took place around the city.

Fifty-five-year-old Crown Prince Akihito and his wife Michiko succeeded to the Chrysanthemum Throne, ushering in the new era name of Heisei. A year later, a small item appeared in an October 2 newspaper, announcing the death of US Air Force General Curtis LeMay, the man who had overseen the 1945 air raid that had resulted in the annihilation of tens of thousands of Tokyo residents. The article noted, without a touch of irony, that in 1964, the Olympic year, the general had been honored with the prestigious First Class of the Order of the Rising Sun for his contribution to postwar Japan's Air Self-Defense Force.

The award had been presented by the emperor himself. The article received little public attention. By then, almost everyone had forgotten the war, and with it, the destruction of Tokyo.

From the enduring Sumida River—the subject of woodblock prints,
kabuki plays and poems over the centuries—is a view of Tokyo Skytree.
(Dreamstime © Torsakarin)

CHAPTER 8

Fault Lines

Infrastructure squeeze – The architectural laboratory –
Another new city – A death cult – 3/11

Peter Ackroyd wrote of London, "The presiding deity of this place has always been money." The same assertion could be made about Tokyo. If you could elect a presiding deity for the city, it might well be Ebisu, the god of commerce and all things leading to profitable conclusions.

Tokyo has never tried to conceal its mercantile character, its worship of wealth, but like Venice, another city founded on trade and cutthroat dealings in the pursuit of lucre, it has glossed over the grubbier aspirations of the procurer with the pretense of being a city of culture. The acquisition of art by private collectors and large corporations during the bubble decade, in fact, was seen as both an investment and a form of prestige.

Despite its showy accrued wealth, Tokyo has not become, in the commonly understood sense, a comfortable city to live in, except for the very affluent. Ordinary people must still endure crowded streets, congested trains and expressways, cramped working conditions, and standards of housing that remain far below those in the West. The spatial inequalities that existed in Edo prevail today, with the well-to-do residing in the more respectable *yamanote* area or choicer parts of the western suburbs, the working and lower middle classes consigned to districts to the north and east of the Sumida River.

In the 1960s, the British architect J. M. Richards described Tokyo as a "terrifying wirescape." If anything, the "wirescape" has intensified in the decades since that remark, with immeasurable voltages of electricity still dangling overhead. The city's asset-driven wealth of the 1980s bankrolled a fresh glut of building and haphazard growth. The new, soaring structures of the seventies and eighties were characterized by irregularity of form, of stepped and sloped buildings, many of them centrally located condominiums called *manshon*, structures with wedge-like upper portions reflecting complex building regulations relating to sunlight access for the mid- and lower-structures around them. In the same way that navigation of the city by low-level waterways was superseded in the early Meiji era by roads that elevated movement around the city, horizontal postwar Tokyo gradually made way for vertical communities inhabiting new private apartment blocks and public housing estates. Residents identify themselves with localities rather than the city in its entirety, so that a citizen of the more desirable western suburbs might never set foot in the crowded downtown districts east of the river or in the congested northern zones. Tokyoites have consigned themselves to partial views of their city.

The richer the capital became, the more brutally indifferent it grew to the needs of the wretched within its midst. The incuriosity of the Tokyoite is not so different from his or her counterpart in London, New York, or Kolkata, which are all home to the same victims of the economy, broken families, ill health, alcoholism, mental distress, dissipation, recidivism, and plain bad luck. In all these cities, poverty is the inevitable progeny of wealth and prodigality. The poor have always existed in this city of inequalities. It is supremely ironic that the most visible residents of Tokyo are the homeless, who lack proper residences. A sense that extreme poverty is contagious prevails. And because the poor signify municipal failure, the authorities have always tried to re-move them from sight, to squeeze them beneath raised express-ways, or among the wild grasses of desolate urban riverbanks. Entire areas inhabited by the homeless have been demolished, as if the districts themselves were culpable, complicit somehow in the act of failure.

At Yasukuni Shrine, in the district of Kudanshita, a different kind of defeat has been reinterpreted as noble failure. Here, the memory of war lingers like an unbidden odor in the long corri-dor of time, one that no amount of scrubbing or disinfecting can expunge. Built in 1869 to enshrine the spirits of Japanese soldiers who died in the service of the emperor, Yasukuni Shrine also in-cludes the remains of men conscripted from Japanese colonies. The shrine's registry lists the names of twelve convicted Class-A war criminals, including former General Tojo Hideki, and two accused war criminals who died in custody before their cases were adjudicated. In 1978, the names were added to those hon-ored at Yasukuni Shrine. Members of the public, who were not consulted, got to read of the action a full year later, when the *Asahi Shimbun* broke the story.

Shrine officials maintain that the souls of the deceased de-serve to be enshrined, as they fell in the service of their country. Some 2.5 million war dead are now honored at Yasukuni, their souls considered divine. For Japanese nationalists, the shrine is homage to the "glorious spirits" who perished serving their coun-try; to the families of victims, the atmosphere of the site has the effect of strong smelling salts, reawakening the horrors of the past. Visits to the site by right-leaning and revisionist members of the government, including a number of prime ministers, have caused outrage among neighboring countries that were victims of Japanese imperialism.

A museum on the grounds of the shrine contains several pe-riod displays, including a steam engine used in the building of the River Kwai death railway, a human-piloted torpedo, and an intact

Zero fighter. A palpable absence of soul-searching or remorse is evident in the texts accompanying the exhibits, which suggest that Japan's wars of the 1930s and 40s were defensive, or, more heroically, crusades to liberate Asia from Western colonization. An unequivocal expression of contrition for the conduct of the Imperial Army during the war is as improbable as a formal apology on the part of the United States government for dropping the atom bombs on Hiroshima and Nagasaki. The layers of silence and amnesia have hardened elsewhere, but at Yasukuni there is a fierce refutation of history akin to an act of injured pride. The tensions over interpretations of history continue to reverberate in the streets of Tokyo, but have little impact on the desirability of living in the capital.

As the national birthrate drops, the population of Tokyo, in fact, grows ever larger. Town planners have been advocating decentralization for decades, with little result. The proposal would see industrial complexes, office and retail areas, university and college campuses, and major commuter destinations relocated closer to residential districts. This nexus of satellite centers positioned at commuter interchanges, rather than overcrowded and disproportionately large central business districts, constitutes the vision for a restructured "multimodal metropolis." Partial implementation of the plan at Minato Mirai 21, a waterfront redevelopment project in Yokohama; the creation of Odaiba, a commercial and recreational zone located on an artificial island in Tokyo Bay; and the addition of a high-rise business, residential, and convention complex at Makuhari, a suburb of Chiba prefecture, have saved distance and time and helped to relieve crowded commuter trains.

The bubble-economy years witnessed an unsurpassed surge in construction. The transformation of Tokyo into an experimental laboratory attracted leading architects from around the world, vindicating the view of Japanese designer Isozaki Arata, when he wrote, "Tokyo is a distressingly ugly city, but it also possesses such mysterious vitality that building in it is a great challenge to an architect." Among those who came to Tokyo to take up that challenge, to add their visions to the dream-like skyline, were such luminaries as Richard Rogers, Hugh Stubbins, Peter Eisenman, Cesar Pelli, Rafael Vinoly, Zaha Hadid, and French designer Philippe Starck.

Major cities are shaped by political and military imperatives, then reshaped by culture. This is spectacularly true of Tokyo. Roppongi is a study in the way architectural projects can utterly transform districts. During the Meiji era, military drill grounds dominated what is now the district of Roppongi after the Imperial Army had taken over a number of daimyo estates in the area. The Japanese army's War College was sited there during World War II, and then the US military used the land during the Occupation. When the grounds were handed back to the Japanese in 1959, the compound was taken over by the Japanese Defense Agency.

The American presence had created a seminal entertainment area, with clubs, bars, and restaurants. The district's transformation from an international but somewhat tawdry area to a nascent cultural zone took place at the turn of the millennium with the creation of the so-called Art Triangle project. This linked the postmodernist steel-and-glass towers of Roppongi Hills Mori Art Museum and Tokyo Midtown—a massive commercial, leisure, and residential center hosting the Suntory Museum of Art—with the National Art Center. Detractors of these over-managed complexes, and of later projects like Toranomon Hills, have pointed out that they are nonessential additions to affluent districts of the city, and that such privileged tracts of costly real estate are of little benefit to more needy parts of the capital. The city's indifference to these gaping disparities is evident, as it always has been, in residential housing conditions. There is a world of difference between well-heeled western districts like Komaba and Denen-chofu, which resemble middle-class English garden suburbs, and the working-class residents living cheek-to-jowl in airless shoe-box apartments in the eastern *shitamachi*.

The artist M. C. Escher or the filmmaker Fritz Lang would have been appalled by the wealth disparities, but intrigued by the asymmetric geometries of present-day Tokyo. Godard's *Alphaville* could easily have been filmed here; Russian director Andrei Tarkovsky's *Solaris*, in fact, was. Ridley Scott, seeking a visually dislocating metaphor for the future, turned his cameras onto neon alleys and disjunctive stacked-up buildings inspired by the districts of Shinjuku and Shibuya for his largely nocturnal sci-fi film *Blade Runner*.

Many Tokyo structures seem unrelated to the things around them. The city is full of such jarring proximities: a police box beside a "soapland" massage salon, a shrine next to a filling station, a cash dispenser abutting the gate to a tea house. Empty space versus mass. The unconsidered acquisition of world symbols, styles, and icons nevertheless has its own charm, as Donald Richie pointed out when he wrote, "There is indeed a real freedom in finding that Doric columns do not mean a bank, nor red roof-tiles, Spain." There is also a certain irony in the fact that many of the city's prominent landmarks are replicas of iconic buildings found in other, mostly Western, cities. Tokyo Station is modeled on Amsterdam's Central Station; Shinjuku's Mode Gakuen Cocoon Tower bears a striking resemblance to Norman Foster's 30 St Mary Axe, better known as the London Gherkin.

The uncoordinated buildings, designed for functional rather than -aesthetic purposes; the concrete-encased riverbanks; the cobwebs of overhead power lines; and the pollarded trees that visitors remark on may not be pretty, but Tokyo is a remarkably well-organized, safe, and clean city with a very special dynamic. The ceaseless movement, the hum and thrum, the white noise that forms a constant soundtrack to Tokyo life is a sign that the city is up and running. Should it ever grow silent, the hush would signal a terminal phase in its existence.

How can the past and present coexist when there appears to be so little connecting space? Part of the answer lies in the distinction the Japanese make between what they call *omote* and *ura*—literally the "front" and "back," but carrying the added and crucial sense of "outside" and "inside"; the publicly displayed and the privately concealed. The *omote-dori*—the wide, public boulevards of the city—contrast with the *ura-dori*, the immensely dense and complex backstreets and alleys. *Omote*, the surface of the modern, often imitative city, dazzles the eyes, deflecting the gaze from the more deeply embedded *ura* aspects. Whether due to natural disaster, aerial bombing, government fiat, the imperatives of business, or individual need, change has become a secular ritual in Tokyo. Habituated to surface change, Tokyoites are nevertheless acutely attuned to the city's underlying structure. Behind the wide boulevards, the modern incarnations of Edo's old firebreaks, you can become lost in a skein of twisting streets and bifurcating lanes. Culture lives in the shadows as well as the bright lights.

Continuities are visible in the circular pattern of the old castle itself, which still exerts an influence on the shape of central Tokyo. The important Yamanote Line, the city's overland rail loop, follows the contours of the moat for a good deal of its length. Subway lines and the JR Chuo Line run alongside the filled-in moat bed at Yotsuya, reappearing beside the moat at Ochanomizu and Kanda. Train lines leaving Tokyo Station also follow the route of the original moat, which has been filled in to provide space for the myriad tracks. Expressways have been absorbed into the original spiral.

Despite radical surface alterations, the streets of Nihonbashi, Ginza, and Shinbashi follow—in broader, more orderly measures—subdivisions established by Edo. The houses have long gone, but the sequence of streets through the Marunouchi and Hibiya districts still follows the routes outlined by older residences. The streets to the north of the Imperial Palace are easily identified on maps of Edo dating from the seventeenth century. And the Tokaido, the old trunk road connecting Edo and Kyoto, still runs south of the city through Takanawa.

Many views made famous through literature and remembrance have vanished, especially those that were once possible to see from the top of street slopes. New vistas, less casually glimpsed, can be enjoyed from skyscraper observation galleries, tower-top bars and restaurants, and new high-rise apartments.

One unique aspect of the city that has not changed is its manner of generational channeling. A typical Tokyoite, or a resident from one of the adjoining prefectures like Saitama or Chiba, is likely to proceed from one district to the next depending on age. The fashion town of Harajuku serves young teens, who will then graduate to the young-adult district of nearby Shibuya. The outlet stores and live houses of Shimokitazawa attract the college crowd; Daikanyama a slightly older, more discerning consumer; chic Aoyama the stylish twenties and thirties shopper; Ginza the middle-aged. Sugamo, an area of temples, Buddhist statues, fortune tellers, purveyors of Chinese medicines, and stonemasons' yards, is an older quarter where the elderly can select their own tombs, and even decide on the wording for inscriptions that will guide them into the afterlife.

Despite the car emissions and smells issuing from the ventilators of fast-food restaurants, present-day Tokyo is not a particularly malodorous place. On the Monday of March 20, 1995, the day before the Spring Equinox, a deadly odor spread like a viscous mist through the subway tunnels of central Tokyo. In retrospect, there were several early indications that an event like the sarin gas attack, which was carried out by members of the Aum Shinrikyo cult on orders given by Asahara Shoko, the group's semi-blind spiritual leader, could take place. The novelist Murakami Haruki recounts witnessing a bizarre sight outside his local train station during Asahara's failed campaign for election to the Lower House of the Japanese Diet. Trucks equipped with powerful speakers played strange music as followers of the cult, dressed in white robes and wearing elephant heads and outlandishly sized Asahara masks, danced on the sidewalks in a scene reminiscent of the "*Ei—janai ka*" excesses witnessed at the closure of the Edo period.

The nerve gas sarin, invented by German scientists in the 1930s, was used in the 1980s by Iraq in its war against Iran and in its genocidal attacks on Kurds. A single drop of sarin, said to be twenty-six more times more lethal than cyanide gas, is enough to kill a healthy adult. In the Tokyo subway assault, the sharpened tips of umbrellas were used to pierce open plastic trash bags containing the gas. One of the leaders of the attack, Hayashi Ikuo, a senior medical doctor, had resigned his prestigious post at the Ministry of Science and Technology to join the cult, which appointed him as Minister of Healing. Hayashi was assigned to release sarin as his train approached Shin-Ochanomizu Station. By the time the bag was disposed of by station attendants, two people had died and 231 passengers had been injured.

Evacuated from the platform at Kasumigaseki Station, passengers lay supine on the ground. Many victims were screaming and sobbing, while others coped with muscular spasms, painfully wheezing lungs, and heart palpitations; still more distressing was the sight of affected people foaming at the mouth, and others who had had spoons placed in their mouths to prevent them from choking on their tongues. The attack killed twelve people, and injured in excess of 5,000.

Hayashi Yasuo, the main perpetrator of the Hibiya Line attack, evaded arrest until December 1996. While on the run, he supposedly took a small Buddhist altar along with him, an object that would assist him in atoning for his sins. One of the most shocking aspects of the attack to the Japanese public was the fact that many members of the millennium cult were scientists and trained technocrats, graduates of the highest educational institutions in the land. In a different age Asahara might have been advocating divination, numerology, or alchemy. In this one, regarded as a holy savant by his followers, he had cast himself as a prophet of death.

Disturbing events continued in the run-up to the new millennium. In the same year as the sarin gas attacks, a mega-earthquake in the city of Kobe killed more than 6,000 people. The government's slow and poorly organized response to the disaster exposed its ineffective emergency network and subsequent inability to deal with major crisis. Two years later, in October, 1998, the press reported that workers at a Japan Railways Tokyo construction site had accidentally disinterred more than a hundred human skulls at the site of the old Kotsukappara Keijo execution grounds. Buried in barrels, the skulls were colored black from the mud. Excavations of a different kind would take place in 2011 in Shinjuku's Toyama neighborhood, at the site of a former army medical school linked to the wartime Unit 731. A former nurse claimed that she and her colleagues had been ordered to bury corpses and body parts in the days following Japan's surrender on August 15, 1945. An investigation was ordered.

The times were clearly out of joint, and Tokyo's leaders were unable to fix them. Self-healing, however, is second nature for Tokyo. In the 1950s, *Harper's* magazine described a newly resurgent Philadelphia as the "Renaissance City of America." Tokyo, with its history of rapid reincarnations, fits the model for a city where reconstruction is synonymous with progress.

Recognition of Tokyo as a world-class city was sought through the creation of iconic architecture, much of it inserted randomly into discordant cityscapes. Oddly, such designs, which would be regarded as disorienting fantasies almost anywhere else, fit into Tokyo's urban mash rather well, at least in the eyes of those who have been in the city long enough to recalibrate their vision.

It is commonplace for buildings that are unprofitable or out of step with the current economic model to be scrapped like used cars or machine parts. Tokyo planners have few qualms about tearing down historic landmarks and replacing them with structures deemed more fitting for the times. Nestled amidst the brilliant surfaces of these newer buildings are increasingly large numbers of CCTV security cameras, and, adding to the surveillance at ground level, a growing contingent of security guards and police, figures in a more brightly illuminated city. It follows that where there is an abundance of light, there must also be pools of darkness.

At 2:49 p.m. on March 11, 2011, even the soundest ferro-concrete structures in Tokyo began to sway and buckle with the effect of an undersea mega-thrust triggering a 9.0 earthquake and tsunami that would slam into the aging Fukushima Daiichi power station along Japan's northeastern coastline, less than 250 kilometers north of the capital. In the worst nuclear accident since Chernobyl, the plant's power system failed, causing the cooling system to shut down, sending reactor cores into meltdown. Several reactor units were heavily damaged by subsequent hydrogen explosions caused by the meltdown.

As radiation spread over a landscape of rice paddies, dairy farms, and fishing villages, efforts by the Tokyo Electric Power Company (TEPCO) at containment involved not only taking measures at the plant itself, but also limiting access to procedural records, downplaying vulnerabilities, and disseminating misinformation. Liquefaction—the breakdown of soil that has not had time to properly solidify—occurred at several points along Tokyo Bay, where areas of newly created reclaimed land are common. If anyone doubted the stability of reclaimed land, which is made of sand from dredging, soil removed from building sites, and waste materials, the liquefaction and subsidence of roads and private homes along sections of Tokyo Bay like Urayasu served as an ominous warning.

Charles Beard, reflecting on the failure of the reconstruction plan that followed the 1923 earthquake, expressed doubts about the ability of those in authority to carry out a "comprehensive scheme of city planning in the face of organized, short-sighted

CHAPTER 8

private interests and political ineptitude." Almost a century on, many of the helpless and dispossessed victims of the 3/11 calamity, shaken by the lack of oversight and emergency planning on the part of the government and the nuclear industry, might legitimately ask if anything has really changed.

It will be decades before towns and villages located near the stricken plant are habitable, ancestral farmland fit to repossess. Dismantling the plant will require the removal of molten fuel from the reactors. The decommissioning process, which could take decades, and place a massive economic burden on the country, has been plagued by the ongoing leakage of radioactive water, inadequate risk management, negligence, and ineptitude.

Water several million times the safety limit for radioactivity has leaked from a storage tank close to the Pacific Ocean. Heavy rains in the wake of typhoons, which are regular and seasonal, have caused massive spikes in the levels of tritium and strontium-90 in radioactive groundwater at the Fukushima Daiichi nuclear plant. What will happen to the severely damaged instillation in the event of another mega-quake?

If nothing else, public awareness and a healthy skepticism of the nuclear industry and its powerful supporters, and of the advisability of constructing reactors on the world's most seismically active terrain, have grown. Antinuclear demonstrations in Tokyo, including one in which more than 60,000 people participated, saw a partial, albeit momentary, return to the activism of the 1960s. Japan has since revised its nuclear regulatory systems, but the collusive circle of politicians, nuclear executives and bureaucrats, known collectively as the "nuclear village," has barely changed. In the days after 3/11, the NASA space satellites that had once registered Tokyo as the brightest city on the globe transmitted images of a much-dimmed capital.

Despite being severely shaken, Tokyo was largely spared, though the empty reassurances of TEPCO's senior management, disseminated by government bodies and a compliant media, belied the fact that the metropolis was assuredly threatened. Had radiation spread to the city, more than 30 million people would have had to be evacuated. This would have effectively signified the collapse of the modern Japanese state as we know it.

More disasters are imminent, and nigh impossible to predict. One might just as well consult one of the many fortunetellers who set up their small tables and paper lanterns on the night pavements of the city, offering to read the destinies of passersby. A lack of faith in predictive accuracy was apparent in the reaction to an interpretation of the 3/11 disaster made by a former governor of Tokyo, Ishihara Shintaro. Echoing the superstitions of a former age, he declared that the Fukushima catastrophe was an instance of *tenbatsu* (divine punishment) for Japan's lapse into materialism. Reflecting a more informed age, the observation was not well received.

The Rainbow Bridge spans Tokyo Bay from Shibaura Wharf to the artificial island of Odaiba. Its completion in 1993 fostered the development of the Odaiba waterfront. (Dreamstime © Pigprox)

AFTERWORD
Plural Zones

Those who try to predict the future of modern metropolises are apt to end up as superannuated Cassandras. The study of past occurrences and portents as a means to understanding the nature of future events—and perhaps of managing them—can be traced to the use of oracle bones for divination in ancient China, the omen tablets of Babylon, and the dialectical materialism practiced by Marx, Engels, and Lenin.

The inaccuracy of such methods may be manifest, the imprecision of engaging in speculative mapping of the future obvious, but even in such an unreadable city as Tokyo, there are trend lines. The fact that a thousand years ago, three of the world's largest cities—Palermo, Seville, and Cordoba—were Muslim counts for little today. Facts do not always carry relevance in the long view of history, but it is significant that Tokyo is now the world's largest metropolis. Other cities midwifed by great cultures may have receded, crumbled into the sand like Leptis Magna, or become architectural artifacts, but Tokyo's stock has risen, invigorated by each of its transformations. There is no reason to suggest an end to the hybrid urbanism that makes the city such an electrifying place to be.

Tokyo has done little to halt the obliteration of history. In a way it is the perfect contemporary city, one that has triumphed over the past by putting history at the rear end of time, and then getting on with the present. A tendency to eviscerate or conceal the material past in favor of an infinite number of alternative futures is no longer confined to Japanese cities. Only a few decades ago, the tallest buildings in London were its church spires. That notion of the skyline as celestial died with the construction of the blandly designed Millbank Tower and the even more conspicuous 1965 Post Office Tower, a structure whose height surpassed Saint Paul's Cathedral. Today many of London's architectural monuments are overshadowed by commercial and residential blocks. In the ancient city of Mecca, where you might suppose Saudi orthodoxy would cherish the past, the residence of Khadijah, the Prophet Muhammad's first wife, has been converted into a block of toilets; the home of Abu Bakr, a close friend of the prophet and Islam's first caliph, was bulldozed to make way for the construction of the Makkah Hilton Hotel.

Change is not confined to the surface. An entire sub-basement city is emerging as Tokyo digs deeper into the earth in search of new ways to achieve decongestion. The inner-city substrata associated with subway lines, sewage channels, and underground streams is being augmented with gleaming malls, restaurants, and cafés. With a byzantine network of shopping tunnels already in place beneath Tokyo Station and more excavations planned, a large proportion of residents from now on will be negotiating an entire sub-basement city.

Tokyo's underground development began in 1927, with the opening of the Ginza Line subway connecting Asakusa with Ueno Station. By 1930, the first underground shops appeared in Ueno Station. The subway system has almost reached capacity, with concern periodically raised about the wisdom of undermining the city's already unstable foundations. In many ways, the system is laudable. It maximizes available space; unlike the New York or Paris undergrounds, every crevice is lit up with bright lights, with no disused corners or areas of darkness visible from the platforms. Tokyo is the exception, though, among large international cities, for not having an all-night transportation system. The Tokyo Metro and metropolitan government-managed stations extend to more than 280 sites and carry more than eight million passengers a day. The lines undulate above and below each other, carefully avoiding other infrastructure such as sewage, electric, and gas pipes; underground parking lots; and communication cables. At the larger subway complexes, lines are separated by just a hand's breadth: in Shinjuku-Sanchome Station, the Fukutoshin Line is a mere 11 centimeters above the Toei Shinjuku Line that runs on the lower level.

In European cities like Barcelona and Frankfurt, freeways were long ago banished to the perimeters; in Tokyo, they penetrate the very center of the metropolis. In an effort to relieve congestion and promote traffic circulation, more expressway offshoots have been grafted onto the existing system in an operation resembling a multiple heart bypass. A plan is gaining traction to rid the city of aging elevated sections of its Metropolitan Expressway by constructing a highway network some 40 meters underground. The existing highway, almost a third of which is more than fifty years old and not quakeproof, was constructed in great haste to meet the 1964 Olympic deadline. By 1967, the elevated sections of the system ran to 32.5 kilometers; today the Metropolitan Expressway stretches more than 300 kilometers. The new scheme would include a long-cherished plan to place a 2-kilometer section of expressway that currently runs directly above the landmark Nihonbashi bridge below ground.

The dangers of such a confined, perpetually congested system would be compounded by unacceptably high levels of nitrogen-oxide emissions. The theory that the magnitude of an earthquake diminishes with depth is a convincing argument for a subterranean road system, but the follies of hasty, ill-conceived construction are evident inside the Sendagaya Tunnel, a section of road laid in 1964. For drivers who claim to have witnessed the occasional sighting of a long-haired female ghost hanging upside-down from the ceiling, the poltergeist's propensity to drop down on cars with a sickly thud highlights the imprudence of building

such a tunnel beneath a cemetery. In 2014, underground congestion forced developers to divert a section of a 900-meter tunnel in
Minato ward through the basement floor of a fifty-two-story skyscraper in the commercial and residential compound of Toranomon Hills. With the Tokyo metro turning into a hollowed-out
complex of malls and tunnels brushing against the footings of
ever-taller skyscrapers, few planners appear to be considering
the probability of subsidence, or even sinkholes.

A dome of heat hangs over the pressurized city in the summer months, pressing exhaust fumes into its living and working
quarters. The national population density will continue to decline while that of Tokyo grows, highlighting the disproportion-
alities that have long characterized the city. Temperatures will
continue to rise, not simply because of the massive amounts of
energy needed to illuminate the city, but from sheer body heat.
At its densest, Tokyo can resemble Kolkata, albeit far more self-
disciplined and efficiently run.

The density of the city and its inconceivable number of residents make it possible to spend your entire life in Tokyo without
ever glimpsing the ocean. You may not even sense the sea, living
behind the phalanx of towers that line the bay area and impede
the relieving breezes that might circulate through the city. Satellite images of Tokyo show a land mass leached of color. Whereas
30 percent of London is set aside for parks and gardens, Tokyo
devotes a meager 5 percent. Thermograph maps of central Tokyo
illustrate the benefits of greenery, with residential blocks near
large gardens and parks registering cooler temperatures than the
superheated congestion of districts and neighborhoods where
most people live and work.

Typically, such unchecked development leads to grave social
and structural concerns. Miraculously, Tokyo has managed to
avoid many of the ill effects of intense urbanization, and can boast
an efficient public transportation system, friendly neighborhoods,
and a relatively low crime rate. It is a safe city to walk in, even at

night. What is remarkable about contemporary Tokyo is that, despite its bewildering complexity, the city manages to function as a single, stable organism. The notion, however, of what Edward Seidensticker called a "single, concentrated orthodoxy" no longer exists. That is not to say that Tokyo is anywhere near becoming an embryonic version of Berlin or Dubai. Tokyo is a cosmopolitan city, but few of its inhabitants are cosmopolitan. The prospect of a more heterogeneous Tokyo is not universally welcomed. There are many who equate it with poisoning the well. Racial tensions are inevitable, but the kind of riots associated with the council estates of London or the *banlieues* of Paris are improbable.

Sooner or later the city will have to face up to its self-evident plurality, to the legion of foreign managers, entrepreneurs, and teachers; the Indians who live in the low-rent ward of Edogawa; the Chinese who have moved into Ikebukuro; the American executive class that has made Minato ward its home; the Nigerian club and bar owners and Russian hostesses of districts like Roppongi; and a service sector that, constituting a new, largely powerless underclass, works as carers, cooks, waiters, dishwashers, convenience-store clerks, factory hands, bar hostesses, escorts, bouncers, musicians, entertainers, masseurs, and street touts. These men and women from West Africa, Southeast Asia, Brazil, India, Asian Russia, Belarus, and Poland are not phantoms, although many of them, too poor to enjoy its amenities, are living in the city but are not a part of it. A city that has denied its diversity will have to accept that it is already a de facto polyglot entity, and draw strength and inspiration from this new age of multicultural urbanism.

Like American cinema audiences, the Japanese appear to enjoy fantasies about their own oblivion. A character in the popular animation series *Tokyo Babylon* says, "Even now I love Tokyo, just as it is. Where else in the world do so many people savor their own descent into destruction?" It is easy to be apocryphal, but one thing that almost everyone agrees on is the imminence of catastrophe in the form of a long-overdue mega-quake. Whether it is conditioned resignation or a case of sangfroid, few Tokyoites let the future prey on their minds. The Japanese may be forgiven their infant-like preference for the cute and sentimental, living as they do in a country where reality comes crashing through windows and ceilings, heaving up from beneath floorboards with unbidden, life-devouring force.

The fate of the city balances on the unspeakable whims of geotectonic forces. Tokyo occupies a singularly vulnerable location, sitting as it does above the Eurasian tectonic plate, which is superimposed upon the Pacific and Philippine Sea plates. This convergence point between the oceanic and continental plates eventually causes tectonic volatility, resulting in earthquakes, volcanoes, and tsunami. Along with the Osaka–Kobe belt and China's Pearl River Delta, Tokyo is ranked the world's most risk-prone metropolitan area. In the absence of any coherent strategy to counter the threat of a major earthquake, and with a reliable chain of command lacking, immeasurable loss of life and damage to property are inevitable.

Centuries of industrious land reclamation have extended the Tokyo shoreline by more than a kilometer. This spongy, unstable base now forms much of the bay area waterfront, as well as a number of artificial islands, deep land incursions contingent with the Tama and Arakawa rivers, and swaths of newly formed residential plots. Liquefaction in these areas is a probability. Computer models suggest that zones prone to liquefaction are not just the doomed eastern suburbs, but also the commercial districts of Marunouchi; Kabutocho, where the stock exchange resides; and the Ginza. Compacted soil in these zones was buried at a depth of thirty to sixty meters, far below the levels of the foundations of the majority of buildings constructed there. The western reaches of Suruga Bay, the most vulnerable impact point for shockwaves, is an intensely developed area of factories, chemical plants, warehouses, gas tanks, oil refineries, and other highly flammable installations that will add fuel to the destruction.

Between the sleek showcase skyscrapers and more recent constructions, which building companies claim are earthquake-proof, are hundreds of thousands of aged structures made of hastily slapped-up plywood surfaced with mortar. This residential mulch will crumble like a stale biscuit before turning into a sea of splintered wood. Shattered fragments from plate glass and neon lighting will rain down onto fleeing or huddled pedestrians, dislodged billboards will turn into guillotines, heavy equipment and light fixtures in offices will collapse, the chemical components of modern surfaces and furniture will be released, liquid petroleum gas tankers will be abandoned in the streets to await ignition, elevators will jam with the first shudders, random explosions create columns of noxious black smoke, and fallen utility poles and stranded traffic will impede emergency services. Exit routes from the city will be blocked by fires, piles of debris, and collapsing bridges. Households where electrical appliances, LPG heaters, gas ranges, and oil stoves are in constant use will have just seconds to switch off these amenities. Port facilities located in the dock areas will be disabled. Roughly 70 percent of Tokyo water mains are said to be unprepared for a major quake.

In accord with the fate of the less affluent from time immemorial, the residents of the lowland eastern districts of the city will be the worst afflicted, with less damage likely in western Tokyo, with its higher elevations and more contemporary infrastructure. The eastern denizens of the city—with their narrow roads, alleys, absence of firebreaks, and relatively large number of wooden homes—are largely built on alluvial soil, which magnifies earthquakes. Large portions of eastern Tokyo lie at sea level; some districts are as much as four meters below it. In districts like Kanegafuchi and Kyojima, which are sited on level ground between the Sumida and Arakawa rivers, fire trucks will find it virtually impossible to access homes jammed into residential blocks that, eschewing a grid system, follow the random contours of former rice-paddies, while roads meander above channels and conduits once used to irrigate farmland.

The disproportionate influence Tokyo exerts on national affairs, the economy, and culture suggests that the effects of the next earthquake will be far more paralyzing than the last one. Despite the death toll and cost of rebuilding the city in 1923, the global repercussions of the disaster were minimal. The effect of a quake now would be felt worldwide within minutes. The over-concentration of the nation's senior politicians; business, industrial, and high-tech leaders; educators; journalists; and researchers inside a tiny central geographical zone presents a colossal security problem. An annihilation of human and material resources would be an unprecedented national disaster. The only way for Tokyo to survive is to shrink, to decentralize.

And yet the city keeps growing. In the midst of this most vulnerable of world cities, Tokyo Skytree, a 634-meter structure with a narrow, gravity-defying base, is a symbol of either extraordinary optimism or resurgent hubris. The phenomenal popularity of the tower, the city's tallest metaphor, cannot allay the feeling that it represents an already-obsolescent concept of the future.

Tokyoites have always lived with a sense of imminent calamity. It has never stopped them from enjoying the life of their city, the roaring maw of activity, to its fullest. In some respects, Tokyo, a city hardened by the violence inflicted upon it, has evolved into a virtually indestructible organism. The irrepressible optimism of the Tokyoite interprets shabby and crowded conditions with a homely, downtown nostalgia; views the razing of community blocks as progress; and sees bright opportunities in the spaces left by the evisceration of history. Characterized by movement and indeterminacy, the metropolis is a palimpsest upon which its story can be rewritten any number of times. When the Tokyo stock exchange opened in Kabutocho in 1878, the day's transactions came to an end when the last strands of a length of suspended rope sputtered into ash. The following day the process was repeated.

Tokyo today bears as little resemblance to its Edo-period incarnation—or even its Meiji-era self—as the mega-skyscrapers of Dubai do its crumbling sand medinas. Without the mnemonic benefits of heritage buildings, one becomes fixated on the present, with little time for the past. Time itself, of course, does not decompose, but everything subject to its tyranny does. Tokyo's answer to dissolution and erosion is self-transformation. In this world of impermanence and change, it is enough that the emblematic value of a historical edifice or district be preserved in name only.

Tokyo's aversion to inertia and desuetude, its infatuation with modernity, is reflected in a vastly different city concept whereby perpetuation is achieved not by preservation, but renewal. The wrecking ball serves as a metronome for this provisional city. If Tokyo is unable to peer at its history in the mirror, it is because its surface is so clouded with building dust. Its inhabitants consent to perpetual change because they are convinced that the past can be vastly improved upon; hence the abiding faith in the totemic power of modernity. One suspects that the reason they remain in such a crowded, combustible city is less the prospect of wealth accumulation than the opportunity to be participants in modernity itself.

The Buddhism that the nation putatively ascribes to teaches that the material world is an illusion, that desire and craving are the cause of anguish and unhappiness. The faith's doctrine of impermanence—that nothing endures, that attachments are temporary—achieves immense traction in this worldly, acquisitive city, where excavations of the past reveal little beneath the lava flow of history.

In its severest winters, when ice and frost grip the early-morning city, you can still walk to the old pond in Hibiya Park, with its fountain and oxidized bronze statue of a crane, wings adorned with graceful icicles, and see that rarest of things in Tokyo: a monument frozen in time.

Unlike the aged cities of Europe, however, it is perpetual change that sustains the pullulating life of this most easterly of capitals. Tokyo, it seems, does not need a past for its future to flourish.

Bibliography

Allinson, G. D. *Suburban Tokyo: A Comparative Study in Politics and Social Change*. Berkeley: University of California Press, 1979.

Ashihara, Yoshinobu. *The Hidden Order: Tokyo through the Twentieth Century*. Tokyo: Kodansha International, 1989.

Barr, Pat. *The Coming of the Barbarians*. London: Macmillan, 1967.

———. *The Deer Cry Pavilion: A Story of Westerners in Japan, 1868–1905*. New York: Macmillan, 1968.

Benfey, Christopher. *The Great Wave*. New York: Random House, 2003.

Bestor, Theodore C. *Neighborhood Tokyo*. Stanford, CA: Stanford University Press, 1989.

———. *Tsukiji: The Fish Market At The Center of the World*. Berkeley, CA: University of California Press, 2004.

Bird, Isabella. *Unbeaten Tracks in Japan*. New York: G.P. Putnam's Sons, 1880.

Birnbaum, Phyllis. *Modern Girls, Shining Stars, the Skies of Tokyo*. New York: Columbia University Press, 1999.

Bodart-Bailey, Beatrice M. *The Dog Shogun: The Personality and Policies of Tokugawa Tsunayoshi*. Honolulu: University of Hawai'i Press, 2006.

Brinckmann, Hans. *Showa Japan: The Post-War Golden Age and Its Troubled Legacy*. Tokyo: Tuttle Publishing, 2008.

Buruma, Ian. *A Japanese Mirror: Heroes and Villains of Japanese Culture*. London: Penguin Books, 1985.

———. *Inventing Japan*. New York: Modern Library, 2003.

Cybriwsky, Roman. *Tokyo*. London: Belhaven Press, 1991.

de Becker, J. E. *The Nightless City, or the History of the Yoshiwara Yukwaku*. Tokyo: ICG Muse, 1899.

Dore, R. P. *City Life in Japan: A Study of a Tokyo Ward*. Berkeley, CA: University of California Press, 1958.

Dunn, J, Charles. *Everyday Life in Traditional Japan*. Tokyo: Charles E. Tuttle Company, 1972.

Enbutsu, Sumiko. *Discover Shitamachi: A Walking Guide to the Other Tokyo*. Tokyo: Shitamachi Times Inc., 1984.

Ernst, Earle. *The Kabuki Theater*. Honolulu: University of Hawai'i Press, 1974.

Finn, Dallas. *Meiji Revisited: The Sites of Victorian Japan*. Tokyo: Weatherhill, Inc., 1995.

Fowler, Edward. *San'ya Blues: Laboring Life in Contemporary Tokyo*. Ithaca, NY: Cornell University Press, 1996.

Friedman, Mildred, ed. *Tokyo: Form and Spirit*. Minneapolis: Harry N. Abrams, Inc., 1986.

Gerster, Robin. *Legless in Ginza: Orienting Japan*. Melbourne: Melbourne University Press, 1999.

Greenfeld, Karl Taro. *Speed Tribes: Days and Nights with Japan's Next Generation*. New York: Harper Perennial, 1994.

Guest, Harry. *Traveller's Literary Companion, Japan*. Lincolnwood, IL: Passport Books, 1995.

Guillain, Robert. *I Saw Tokyo Burning*. London: John Murray, 1981.

Hane, Mikiso, ed. and trans. *Reflections on the Way to the Gallows: Rebel Women in Prewar Japan*. Berkeley, CA: University of California Press, 1988.

Harvey, Robert. *American Shogun: MacArthur, Hirohito and the American Duel with Japan*. London: John Murray, 2006.

Hayashi, Tadahiko. *Kastori*. Tokyo: Pie, 2007.

Hibbett, Howard. *The Floating World in Japanese Fiction*. Oxford: Oxford University Press, 1959.

Ishiguro, Kazuo. *An Artist of the Floating World*. London: Faber and Faber, 1986.

Ito, Ken K. *Visions of Desire: Tanizaki's Fictional Worlds*. Stanford, CA: Stanford University Press, 1991.

Jinnai, Hidenobu. *Tokyo: A Spatial Anthology*. Berkeley, CA: University of California Press, 1995.

Jones, H. J. *Live Machines: Hired Foreigners and Meiji Japan*. Vancouver: University of British Columbia Press, 1980.

Kawaguchi, Matsutaro. *Stories from a Tokyo Teahouse*. Tokyo: Tuttle Publishing, 2006.

Kern, Adam L. *Manga from the Floating World: Comic-book Culture and the Kibyoshi of Edo Japan*. Boston: Harvard University Asia Center, 2006.

Large, Stephen S. *Emperors of the Rising Sun: Three Biographies*. Tokyo: Kodansha International, 1997.

Lee, Frank H. *Tokyo Calendar*. Tokyo: Hokuseido Press, 1934.

Mansfield, Stephen. *Tokyo: A Cultural and Literary History*. Oxford: Signal Books/Oxford University Press, 2009.

———. *Top 10 Tokyo*. London: Dorling Kindersley Limited, 2010.

McClain, James L. *Japan: A Modern History*. New York: W. W. Norton & Company, 2002.

Meech-Pekarik, Julia. *The World of the Meiji Print: Impressions of a New Civilization*. Tokyo: Weatherhill, 1986.

Milton, Giles. *Samurai William: The Englishman Who Opened Japan*. New York: Penguin Books, 2002.

Minear, Richard H. *The Scars of War: Tokyo during World War II: Writings of Takeyama Michio*. Lanham, MD: Rowman & Littlefield, 2007.

———. *The Tokyo War Crimes Trial*. Princeton, NJ: Princeton University Press, 1971.

Mitchell, David. *Number9Dream*. London: Hodder and Stoughton, 2001.

Naito, Akira, and Kazuo Hozumi. *Edo, the City that Became Tokyo: An Illustrated History*. Tokyo: Kodansha International, 2003.

Nakamura, Mitsuo. *Contemporary Japanese Fiction, 1926–1968*. Tokyo: Kokusai Bunka Shinkokai, 1969.

Nathan, John. *Mishima: A Biography*. Boston: Da Capo Press, 1974.

Nishida, Kazuo. *Storied Cities of Japan*. Tokyo: Weatherhill, 1963.

Nishiyama, Matsunosuke. *Edo Culture: Daily Life and Diversions in Urban Japan, 1600–1868*. Honolulu: University of Hawai'i Press, 1997.

Peace, David. *Tokyo Year Zero*. London: Faber and Faber, 2007.

Popham, Peter. *Tokyo: The City at the End of the World*. Tokyo: Kodansha International, 1985.

Richie, Donald. *A Hundred Years of Japanese Film*. Tokyo: Kodansha International, 2001.

———. *The Honorable Visitors*. Tokyo: ICG Muse, Inc., 2001.

———. *Tokyo: A View of the City*. London: Reaktion Books, 1999.

———. *Tokyo Megacity*. Tokyo: Tuttle Publishing, 2010.

Rogers, Lawrence. *Tokyo Stories: A Literary Stroll*. Berkeley, CA: University of California Press, 2002.

Sacchi, Livio. *Tokyo: City and Architecture*. Milan: Skira, 2004.

Saga, Junichi. *Confessions of a Yakuza*. Tokyo: Kodansha International, 1991.

Schreiber, Mark. *The Dark Side: Infamous Japanese Crimes And Criminals*. Tokyo: Kodansha International, 2001.

Seidensticker, Edward. *Low City, High City*. Tokyo: Tuttle, 1983.

———. *Tokyo Rising*. Tokyo: Tuttle, 1991.

———. *Kafu the Scribbler: The Life and Writings of Nagai Kafu, 1879–1959*. Stanford, CA: Stanford University Press, 1965.

Seigle, Cecilia, Tim Clark, Alfred Marks, and Amy Reigle Newland. *A Courtesan's Day: Hour by Hour*. Amsterdam: Hotei Publishing, 2004.

Silverberg, Miriam. *Erotic, Grotesque, Nonsense: The Mass Culture of Japanese Modern Times*. Berkeley, CA: University of California Press, 2006.

Smith, Martin Cruz. *December 6*. New York: Simon & Schuster, 2002.

Stokes, Henry Scott. *The Life and Death of Yukio Mishima*. New York: Farrar, Straus and Giroux, 1974.

Tanizaki, Junichiro. *Childhood Years*. Tokyo: Kodansha International, 1988.

Tatsumi, Yoshihiro. *Abandon the Old in Tokyo*. Montreal: Drawn & Quarterly, 2012.

Waley, Paul. *Fragments of a City*. Tokyo: The Japan Times, 1992.

———. *Tokyo: City of Stories*. Tokyo: Weatherhill, 1991.

Whitney, Clara A. *Clara's Diary: An American Girl in Meiji Japan*. Tokyo: Kodansha International, 1979.

Whiting, Robert. *Tokyo Underworld*. New York: Vintage Books, 1999.

Wildes, H. E. *Typhoon in Tokyo: The Occupation and Its Aftermath*. New York: Macmillan, 1954.

Worrall, Julian and Golani Erez Solomon. *21st Century Tokyo: A Guide to Contemporary Architecture*. Tokyo: Kodansha International, 2010.

Yamamoto, Kenji. *Tokyo: The Making of a Metropolis*. Tokyo: Tokyo Metropolitan Government, 1993.

Filmography

Tokyo March (1929). Directed by Mizoguchi Kenji.

Stray Dog (1949). Directed by Kurosawa Akira.

Tokyo Story (1953). Directed by Ozu Yasujiro.

Godzilla (1954). Directed by Honda Ishiro.

House of Bamboo (1955). Directed by Samuel Fuller.

A Crowded Streetcar (1957). Directed by Ichikawa Kon.

When a Woman Ascends the Stairs (1960). Directed by Naruse Mikio.

Tokyo Olympiad (1965). Directed by Ichikawa Kon.

You Only Live Twice (1967). Directed by Lewis Gilbert.

Diary of a Shinjuku Thief (1969). Directed by Oshima Nagisa.

Tora San: It's Tough Being a Man (1969). Directed by Yamada Yoji.

The Yakuza (1974). Directed by Sidney Pollack.

Tokyo-Ga (1985). Directed by Wim Wenders.

Akira (1988). Directed by Otomo Katsuhiro.

Tokyo Pop (1988). Directed by Fran Rubei Kuzui.

Grave of the Fireflies (1988). Directed by Takahata Isao.

Neon Genesis Evangelion (1995). Directed by Anno Hideaki.

Enlightenment Guaranteed (1999). Directed by Doris Dorrie.

Millennium Actress (2001). Directed by Kon Satoshi.

Lost in Translation (2003). Directed by Sofia Coppola.

Nobody Knows (2004). Directed by Koreeda Hirokazu.

Always: Sunset on Third Street (2005). Directed by Yamazaki Takashi.

Babel (2006). Directed by Alejandro Gonzalez Inarritu.

Yasukuni (2007). Directed by Ling Yi.

Tokyo Magnitude 8.0 (2009). Directed by Tachibana Masaki and Takahashi Natsuko.

Enter The Void (2009). Directed by Gaspar Noe.

Map of the Sounds of Tokyo (2009). Directed by Isabel Coixet.

Emperor (2012). Directed by Peter Webber.

Index